RESUMES
FOR
FORMER
MILITARY
PERSONNEL

RESUMES
FOR
FORMER
MILITARY
PERSONNEL

The Editors of
VGM Career Books

Second Edition, With Sample Cover Letters

VGM Career Books

Chicago   New York   San Francisco   Lisbon   London   Madrid   Mexico City
Milan   New Delhi   San Juan   Seoul   Singapore   Sydney   Toronto

Library of Congress Cataloging-in-Publication Data

Resumes for former military personnel / the editors of VGM Career
Books. — 2nd ed.
    p.   cm. — (VGM professional resumes series)
  Rev. ed. of: Resumes for ex-military personnel. c1996
  ISBN 0-658-01104-9
  1. Resumes (Employment).   2. Cover letters.
3. Veterans—Employment.   4. Retired military personnel—Employment.
I. VGM Career Books (Firm)   II. Title: Resumes for ex-military personnel.
III. Series.
  HF5383 .R4374   2001
  808'.06665—dc21
                                              00-53374

*We would like to acknowledge the assistance of Luisa Gerasimo
in the compiling and editing of this book.*

VGM Career Books
A Division of The McGraw·Hill Companies

First published as *Resumes for Ex-Military Personnel* in 1996 by VGM Career Horizons.

2 3 4 5 6 7 8 9 0 VLP VLP 0 5 4 3 2 1

ISBN 0-658-01104-9

This book was set in Minion by City Desktop Productions
Printed and bound by Vicks Lithograph

This book is printed on acid-free paper.

Contents

RESUMES
FOR
FORMER
MILITARY
PERSONNEL

Introduction

Your resume is the first impression you give a prospective employer. Though you may be articulate, intelligent, and charming in person, a poor resume may prevent you from ever having the opportunity to demonstrate your interpersonal skills, because it may prevent you from being called for an interview. While few people have ever been hired solely on the basis of their resume, a well-written, well-organized resume can go a long way toward helping you land an interview. Your resume's main purpose is to get you that interview. The rest is up to you and the employer. If you both feel that you are right for the job and the job is right for you, chances are you will be hired.

A resume must catch the reader's attention yet still be easy to read and to the point. Resume styles have changed over the years. Today, brief and focused resumes are preferred. Employers no longer have the patience, or the time, to review several pages of solid type. A resume should be only one page long, if possible, and never more than two pages. Time is a precious commodity in today's business world; the resume that is concise and straightforward will usually be the one that gets noticed.

Let's not make the mistake, though, of assuming that writing a brief resume means that you can take less care in preparing it. A successful resume takes time and thought, but if you are willing to make the effort, the rewards are well worth it. Think of your resume as a sales brochure with the product being you. You want to sell yourself to a prospective employer. This book is designed to help you prepare a resume that will further your career—to land that next job, or first job, or to return to the workforce after years of absence. So, read on. Make the effort and then reap the rewards that a strong resume can bring to your career. Let's get to it!

The Elements of a Good Resume

A winning resume is made from the elements that employers are most interested in seeing when reviewing a job applicant. These basic elements are the key ingredients of a successful resume and become the section headings of your resume. The following is a list of elements that may be used in a resume. Some are essential, some are optional. We will be discussing these in this chapter to give you a better understanding of each element's role in the makeup of your resume:

1. Heading

2. Objective

3. Work Experience

4. Education

5. Honors

6. Activities

7. Certificates and Licenses

8. Professional Memberships

9. Special Skills

10. Personal Information

11. References

The first step in preparing your resume is to gather information about yourself and your past accomplishments. Later you will refine this information, rewrite it in the most effective language, and organize it into an attractive layout. First, let's take a look at each of these important elements individually.

Heading

The heading may seem to be a simple enough element in your resume, but be careful not to take it lightly. The heading should be placed at the top of your resume and should include your name, home address, and telephone numbers. If you can take calls at your current place of business, include your business number, since most employers will attempt to contact you during the business day. If this is not possible, purchase an answering machine that allows you to retrieve your messages while you are away from home. This way you can make sure you don't miss important phone calls. *Always* include your phone number on your resume. It is crucial that prospective employers are able to have immediate contact with you when they need to.

Objective

When seeking a particular career path, it is important to list a job objective on your resume. This statement helps employers determine the direction that you see yourself heading, so that they can determine whether your goals are in line with the position available. The objective is normally one sentence long and describes your employment goals clearly and concisely. See the sample resumes in this book for examples of objective statements.

The job objective will vary depending on your personality, your career field, and your goals. It can be either specific or general, but it should always be to the point.

In some cases, this element is not necessary, but it is usually a good idea to include your objective. It gives your potential employer an idea of where you are coming from and where you want to go.

The objective statement is better left out, however, if you are uncertain of the exact title of the job you seek. In such a case, the inclusion of an overly specific objective statement could result in your not being considered for a variety of acceptable positions; incorporate your job objective into your cover letter instead.

Work Experience

Work experience is arguably the most important element of them all. It will provide the central focus of your resume, so it is necessary that this section be as complete as possible. Only by examining your work experience in depth can you get to the heart of your accomplishments and present them in a way that demonstrates the strength of your qualifications. Of course, someone just out of school will have less work experience than someone who has been working for a number of years, but the amount of information isn't the most important thing—how it is presented, and how it highlights you as a person and as a worker will be what counts mosts.

As you work on this section of your resume, be aware of the need for accuracy. Include all necessary information about each of your jobs, including job title, dates, employer, city, state, responsibilities, special projects, and accomplishments. Be sure to list only company accomplishments for which you were directly responsible. If you haven't participated in any special projects, that's all right—this area may not be relevant to certain jobs.

The most common way to list your work experience is in *reverse chronological order.* In other words, start with your most recent job and work your way backward. This way your prospective employer sees your current (and often most important) job before seeing your past jobs. Your most recent position, if the most important, should also be the one that includes the most information as compared to your previous positions.

The following worksheets will help you gather information about your past jobs.

WORK EXPERIENCE

Job One:

Job Title _____

Dates _____

Employer _____

City, State _____

Major Duties _____

_____

_____

_____

_____

_____

_____

_____

Special Projects _____

_____

_____

Accomplishments _____

_____

_____

_____

_____

_____

_____

Job Two:

Job Title _____

Dates _____

Employer _____

City, State _____

Major Duties _____

_____

_____

_____

_____

_____

_____

_____

Special Projects _____

_____

_____

_____

Accomplishments _____

_____

_____

_____

_____

_____

_____

_____

_____

Job Three:

Job Title _____

Dates _____

Employer _____

City, State _____

Major Duties _____

_____

_____

_____

_____

_____

_____

_____

Special Projects _____

_____

_____

_____

Accomplishments _____

_____

_____

_____

_____

_____

_____

_____

_____

Job Four:

Job Title _____

Dates _____

Employer _____

City, State _____

Major Duties _____

_____

_____

_____

_____

_____

_____

_____

_____

Special Projects _____

_____

_____

_____

Accomplishments _____

_____

_____

_____

_____

_____

_____

_____

_____

Education

Education is the second most important element of a resume. Your educational background is often a deciding factor in an employer's decision to hire you. Be sure to stress your accomplishments in school with the same finesse that you stressed your accomplishments at work. If you are looking for your first job, your education will be your greatest asset, since your work experience will most likely be minimal. In this case, the education section becomes the most important. You will want to include any degrees or certificates you received, your major area of concentration, any honors, and any relevant activities. List your most recent schooling first. If you have completed graduate-level work, begin with that and work in reverse chronological order through your undergraduate education. If you have completed an undergraduate degree, you may choose whether to list your high school experience or not. Do so only if your high school grade point average was well above average.

The following worksheets will help you gather information for this section of your resume. Also included are supplemental worksheets for honors and for activities. Sometimes honors and activities are listed in a section separate from education, most often near the end of the resume.

EDUCATION

School _____

Major or Area of Concentration _____

Degree _____

Dates _____

School Two _____

Major or Area of Concentration _____

Degree _____

Dates _____

Honors

In the honors section, list any awards, honors, or memberships in honorary societies that you have received. Usually these are of an academic nature, but you can also list any honor received for special achievement in sports, clubs, or other school activities. Always include the name of the organization honoring you and the date(s) received. Use the worksheet below to help gather your honors information.

HONORS

Honor One _____

Awarding Organization _____

Date(s) _____

Honor Two _____

Awarding Organization _____

Date(s) _____

Honor Three _____

Awarding Organization _____

Date(s) _____

Honor Four _____

Awarding Organization _____

Date(s) _____

Activities

You may have been active in different organizations or clubs during your years at school; often an employer will look at such involvement as evidence of initiative and dedication. Your ability to take an active role, especially a leadership role, in a group should be included on your resume. Use the worksheet provided to list your activities and accomplishments in this area. In general, you should exclude any organization whose name indicates the race, creed, sex, age, marital status, sexual orientation, or nation of origin of its members.

ACTIVITIES

Organization/Activity _____

Accomplishments _____

_____

_____

Organization/Activity _____

Accomplishments _____

_____

_____

Organization/Activity _____

Accomplishments _____

_____

_____

Organization/Activity _____

Accomplishments _____

_____

_____

As your work experience increases through the years, your school activities and honors will play less of a role in your resume, and eventually you will most likely list only your degree and any major honors you received. As time goes by, your job performance becomes the most important factor to a prospective employer. Your resume should change over the years to reflect this.

Certificates and Licenses

If your chosen career path requires specialized training, you may already have certificates or licenses. You should list these if the job you are seeking requires them and you, of course, have acquired them. If you have applied for a license but have not yet received it, use the phrase "application pending."

License requirements vary by state. If you have moved or are planning to move to another state, check with that state's board or licensing agency for all licensing requirements.

Always be sure that all of the information you list is completely accurate. Locate copies of your certificates and licenses and check the exact date and name of the accrediting agency. Use the following worksheet to list your certificates and licenses.

CERTIFICATES AND LICENSES

Name of License _____

Licensing Agency _____

Date Issued _____

Name of License _____

Licensing Agency _____

Date Issued _____

Name of License _____

Licensing Agency _____

Date Issued _____

Professional Memberships

Another potential element in your resume is a section listing professional memberships. Use this section to list involvement in professional associations, unions, and similar organizations. It is to your advantage to list any professional memberships that pertain to the job you are seeking. Be sure to include the dates of your involvement and whether you took part in any special activities or held any offices within the organization. Use the following worksheet to gather your information.

PROFESSIONAL MEMBERSHIPS

Name of Organization _____

Offices Held _____

Activities _____

Dates _____

Name of Organization _____

Offices Held _____

Activities _____

Dates _____

Name of Organization _____

Offices Held _____

Activities _____

Dates _____

Name of Organization _____

Offices Held _____

Activities _____

Dates _____

Special Skills

The special skills section of your resume is the place to mention any abilities you have that could relate to the job you are seeking. This is the part of your resume where you have the opportunity to demonstrate certain talents and experiences that are not necessarily a part of your educational or work experience. Common examples include fluency in a foreign language or knowledge of a particular computer application.

Special skills can encompass a wide range of your talents—remember to list only skills that relate to the type of work you are looking for.

Personal Information

Some people include personal information on their resumes. This is generally not recommended, but you might wish to include it if you think that something in your personal life, such as a hobby or talent, has some bearing on the position you are seeking. This type of information is often referred to at the beginning of an interview, when it is used as an "icebreaker." Of course, personal information regarding race, creed, sex, age, marital status, sexual orientation, or nation of origin should never appear on any resume.

References

References are not usually listed on the resume, but a prospective employer needs to know that you have references who may be contacted if necessary. All that is necessary to include in your resume regarding references is a sentence at the bottom stating, "References are available upon request," in case a prospective employer requests a list of references. Check with whomever you list to see if it is all right for you to use them as a reference. Forewarn them that they may receive a call regarding a reference for you. This way they can be prepared to give you the best reference possible.

Writing Your Resume

Now that you have gathered all of the information for each of the sections of your resume, it's time to write out each section in a way that will get the attention of whoever is reviewing it. The type of language you use in your resume will affect its success. Translate your information into a language that will cause a potential employer to take notice.

Resume writing is not like expository writing or creative writing. It embodies a functional, direct writing style and focuses on the use of action words. By using action words in your writing, you effectively stress past accomplishments. Action words demonstrate your initiative and highlight your talents. Writing with action words and strong verbs characterizes you to potential employers as an energetic, active person. Remember, your writing is all they know of you until you go in for the interview; your resume will be their first impression.

The following is a list of verbs commonly used in resume writing. Use this list to choose the action words that can help your resume become strong:

administered	billed
advised	built
analyzed	carried out
arranged	channeled
assembled	collected
assumed responsibility	communicated

compiled	maintained
completed	managed
conducted	met with
contacted	motivated
contracted	negotiated
coordinated	operated
counseled	orchestrated
created	ordered
cut	organized
designed	oversaw
determined	performed
developed	planned
directed	prepared
dispatched	presented
distributed	produced
documented	programmed
edited	published
established	purchased
expanded	recommended
functioned as	recorded
gathered	reduced
handled	referred
hired	represented
implemented	researched
improved	reviewed
inspected	saved
interviewed	screened
introduced	served as
invented	served on

sold	tested
suggested	trained
supervised	typed
taught	wrote

Now take a look at the information you put down on the work experience worksheets. Take that information and rewrite it in paragraph form, using verbs to highlight your actions and accomplishments. Let's look at two versions of an example, remembering that what matters here is the writing style, and not the particular job responsibilities given in our sample.

WORK EXPERIENCE
Regional Sales Manager

Manager of sales representatives from seven states. Responsible for twelve food chain accounts in the East. In charge of directing the sales force in planned selling toward specific goals. Supervisor and trainer of new sales representatives. Consulting for customers in the areas of inventory management and quality control.

Special Projects: Coordinator and sponsor of annual food industry sales seminar.

Accomplishments: Monthly regional volume went up twenty-five percent during my tenure while, at the same time, a proper sales/cost ratio was maintained. Customer-company relations improved significantly.

Below is the rewritten version of this information, using action words. Notice how much stronger it sounds.

WORK EXPERIENCE
Regional Sales Manager

Managed sales representatives from seven states. Handled twelve food chain accounts in the eastern United States. Directed the sales force in planned selling toward specific goals. Supervised and trained new sales representatives. Consulted for customers in the areas of inventory management and quality control. Coordinated and sponsored the annual Food Industry Seminar. Increased monthly regional volume twenty-five percent and helped to improve customer-company relations during my tenure.

Another way of constructing the work experience section is by using actual job descriptions. Job descriptions are rarely written using the proper resume language, but they do include all the information necessary to create this section of your resume. Take the description of one of the jobs you are including on your resume (if you have access to it), and turn it into an action-oriented paragraph. Below is an example of a job description followed by a version of the same description written using action words and actual job details. Again, pay attention to the style of writing, as the details of your own work experience will be unique.

WORK EXPERIENCE
Public Administrator I

Responsibilities: Coordinate and direct public services to meet the needs of the nation, state, or community. Analyze problems; work with special committees and public agencies; recommend solutions to governing bodies.

Aptitudes and Skills: Ability to relate to and communicate with people; solve complex problems through analysis; plan, organize, and implement policies and programs. Knowledge of political systems, financial management, personnel administration, program evaluation, and organizational theory.

WORK EXPERIENCE
Public Administrator I

Wrote pamphlets and conducted discussion groups to inform citizens of legislative processes and consumer issues. Organized and supervised twenty-five interviewers. Trained interviewers in effective communication skills.

Now that you have learned how to word your resume, you are ready for the next step in your quest for a winning resume: assembly and layout.

Chapter 3

Assembly and Layout

At this point, you've gathered all the necessary information for your resume, and you've rewritten it using the language necessary to impress potential employers. Your next step is to assemble these elements in a logical order and lay them out on the page neatly and attractively to achieve the desired effect: getting that interview.

Assembly

The order of the elements in a resume makes a difference in its overall effect. Obviously, you would not want to put your name and address in the middle of the resume or your special skills section at the top. You want to put the elements in an order that stresses your most important achievements, not the less pertinent information. For example, if the job you want utilizes training you received in the military, list information about your military career before you list your education. On the other hand, if you have been gainfully employed in civilian life for many years and currently hold an important position in your company, you may want to list your work experience ahead of your military skills, which have become less pertinent with time.

Some elements are always included in your resume, and some are optional. Following is a list of essential and optional elements:

Essential	Optional
Name	Job Objective
Address	Honors
Phone Number	Special Skills
Work Experience	Professional Memberships
Education	Activities
	Certificates and Licenses
	Personal Information
	References Phrase

Your choice of optional sections depends on your own background and employment needs. Always use information that puts you and your abilities in a favorable light. If your honors are impressive, include them in your resume. If your activities in school demonstrate particular talents necessary for the job you are seeking, then allow space for a section on activities. Each resume is unique, just as each person is unique.

Types of Resumes

So far, our discussion about resumes has involved the most common type—the *reverse chronological* resume (see example on page 22), in which your most recent job is listed first and so on. This is the type of resume usually preferred by human resources directors, and it is the one most frequently used. However, in some cases this style of presentation is not the most effective way to highlight your skills and accomplishments.

For someone reentering the workforce after many years or someone looking to change career fields, the *functional resume* may work best (see example on page 23). This type of resume focuses more on achievement and less on the sequence of your work history. In the functional resume, your experience is presented by what you have accomplished and the skills you have developed in your past work.

Assemble a functional resume from the same information you collected for your chronological resume. The main difference lies in how you organize this information. Essentially, the work experience section becomes two sections, with your job duties and accomplishments comprising one section and your employer's name, city, state, your position, and the dates employed making up another section. Place the first section near the top of the resume, just below the job objective section, and call it *Accomplishments* or *Achievements*. The second section, containing the bare essentials of your employment history, should come after the accomplishments section and can be titled *Work Experience* or *Employment History*. The other sections of your resume remain the same. The work experience section is the only one affected in the functional resume. By placing the section that focuses on your achievements first, you draw attention to these achievements. This puts less emphasis on who you worked for and more emphasis on what you did and what you are capable of doing.

For someone changing careers, emphasis on skills and achievements is essential. The identities of previous employers, which may be unrelated to one's new job field, need to be downplayed. The functional resume accomplishes this task. For someone reentering the workforce after many years, a functional resume is the obvious choice. If you lack full-time work experience, you will need to draw attention away from this fact and instead focus on your skills and abilities. Education may play a more important role in this resume.

The type of resume that is right for you depends on your own personal circumstances. It may be helpful to create a chronological *and* a functional resume and then compare the two to find out which is more suitable. The sample resumes found in this book include both chronological and functional resumes. Use these resumes as guides to help you decide on the content and appearance of your own resume.

Layout

Once you have decided which elements to include in your resume and have arranged them in an order that makes sense and emphasizes your achievements and abilities, it is time to work on the physical layout of your resume.

There is no single appropriate layout that applies to every resume, but there are a few basic rules to follow in putting your resume on paper:

1. Leave a comfortable margin on the sides, top, and bottom of the page (usually 1 to 1½ inches).

2. Use appropriate spacing between the sections (usually 2 to 3 line spaces are adequate).

3. Be consistent in the *type* of headings you use for the different sections of your resume. For example, if you capitalize the heading EMPLOYMENT HISTORY, don't use initial capitals and underlining for a heading of equal importance, such as Education.

CHRONOLOGICAL RESUME

RASHEED B. SMITH II
11 Hillcrest Drive • Columbia, SC 29202
(803) 555-1859

EXPERIENCE

1999 - 2002   **Equal Opportunity Program Specialist, U.S. Navy (E-7)**
Classification: Chief Petty Officer
Duties: Served as advisor to officers on equal opportunity matters, provided training in non-discrimination practices, assisted in formulating and revising equal opportunity directives, performed related duties.

1994 - 1999   **Personnelman, U.S. Navy (E-6)**
Classification: Advanced from Personnelman Third Class to Personnelman First Class
Duties: Provided a variety of personnel administration duties.

1993 - 1994   **Seaman, U.S. Navy (E-3)**
Duties: Performed basic seamanship functions.

EDUCATION

B.S.   **University of South Carolina, 1998**
Major: Political Science
Minor: Sociology

Graduate, Defense Equal Opportunity Training Institute, 1997

Completed Navy Instructor Training Program, 1997

REFERENCES

Available on request.

FUNCTIONAL RESUME

William K. Brown
615 Cardinal Drive, Fergus Falls, MN 56537
(218) 555-0464 (voice)
(218) 555-1855 (fax)

Career Objective

A position in surveying or topographic engineering.

Related Skills and Experience

- Highly skilled topographic surveyor with fifteen years' experience in the United States Army.
- Achieved advanced skill level through extensive field experience and Army training courses.
- Thoroughly familiar with the most effective contemporary surveying methods, including use of various types of surveying equipment.

Work Background

As Army topographic surveyor, performed tasks such as the following:

- Recorded topographic survey data
- Operated a variety of survey instruments
- Performed topographic and geodetic computations
- Interpreted maps and aerial photographs
- Perfromed a wide range of computations including horizontal differences, angular closures, and triangulations
- Supervised other workers including topographic instrument repair specialists
- Supervised programming of electronic calculators
- Prepared technical and personnel reports

Training/Education

Completed military training in mathematics, surveying, engineering computations, technical writing, optics, data processing, and related areas.

References Available on Request

4. Always try to fit your resume onto one page. If you are having trouble fitting all your information onto one page, perhaps you are trying to say too much. Edit out any repetitive or unnecessary information, shorten descriptions of earlier jobs, and consider that you may have included too many optional sections. Be ruthless.

Don't let the compulsion to tell every detail about your life prevent you from producing a resume that is simple and straightforward. The more compact your resume, the easier it will be to read and the better the impression it will make for you.

In some cases, the resume will not fit on a single page, even after extensive editing. In such cases, the resume should be printed on two pages so as not to compromise clarity or appearance. Each page of a two-page resume should be marked clearly with your name and the page number, for example, "Judith Ramirez, page 1 of 2." The pages should be stapled together.

Experiment with various layouts until you find one that looks good to you. Always show your final layout to other people and ask them what they like or dislike about it and what impresses them most about your resume. Make sure that is what you want most to emphasize. If it isn't, you may want to consider making changes in your layout until the necessary information is emphasized. Use the sample resumes in this book to get some ideas for laying out your resume.

Putting Your Resume in Print

Your resume should be printed on good quality 8½″ × 11″ bond paper. You want to make as good an impression as possible with your resume; therefore, quality paper is a necessity. If you have access to a word processor with a good printer or know of someone who does, make use of it. Typewritten resumes should be used only when there are no other options available.

After you have produced a clean original, make duplicate copies of it. Usually a copy shop is your best bet for producing copies without smudges or streaks. Have the copy shop use quality bond paper for all copies of your resume, and ask for a sample copy before they run your entire order. After copies are made, check each copy for cleanliness and clarity.

Another, more costly, option is to have your resume typeset and printed by a printer. This provides the most attractive resume of all. If you anticipate needing a lot of copies of your resume, the cost of having it typeset may be justified.

Proofreading

After you have finished typing the master copy of your resume and before you have it copied or printed, thoroughly check it for typing and spelling errors. Have several people read it over just in case you have missed an error. Misspelled words and typing mistakes do not make a good impression on a prospective employer, as they reflect badly on your writing ability and your attention to detail. With thorough and conscientious proofreading, these mistakes can be avoided.

The following are some rules of capitalization and punctuation that may come in handy when proofreading your resume:

RULES OF CAPITALIZATION

- Capitalize proper nouns, such as names of schools, colleges, and universities; names of companies; and brand names of products.

- Capitalize major words in the names and titles of books, tests, and articles that appear in the body of your resume.

- Capitalize words in major section headings of your resume.

- Do not capitalize words just because they seem important.

- When in doubt, consult a manual of style such as *Words into Type* (Prentice Hall) or *The Chicago Manual of Style* (The University of Chicago Press). Your local library can help you locate these and other reference books.

RULES OF PUNCTUATION

- Use a comma to separate words in a series.

- Use a semicolon to separate series of words that already include commas within the series.

- Use a semicolon to separate independent clauses that are not joined by a conjunction.

- Use a period to end a sentence.

- Use a colon to show that examples or details follow that will expand or amplify the preceding phrase.

- Avoid the use of dashes.

- Avoid the use of brackets.

- If you use any punctuation in an unusual way in your resume, be consistent in its use.

- Whenever you are uncertain, consult a style manual.

The Cover Letter

Once your resume has been assembled, laid out, and printed to your satisfaction, the final step before distribution is to write your cover letter. Though there may be instances when you deliver your resume in person, you usually send it through the mail. Resumes sent through the mail always need an accompanying letter that briefly introduces you and your resume. The purpose of the cover letter is to get a potential employer to read your resume, just as the purpose of your resume is to get that same potential employer to call you for an interview.

Like your resume, your cover letter should be clean, neat, and direct. A cover letter usually includes the following information:

1. Your name and address (unless it already appears on your personal letterhead).

2. The date.

3. The name and address of the person and company to whom you are sending your resume.

4. The salutation ("Dear Mr." or "Dear Ms." followed by the person's last name, or "To Whom It May Concern" if you are answering a blind ad).

5. An opening paragraph explaining why you are writing (for example: in response to an ad, the result of a previous meeting, at the suggestion of someone you both know) and indicating that you are interested in the job being offered.

6. One or two more paragraphs that tell why you want to work for the company and what qualifications and experience you can bring to that company.

7. A final paragraph that closes the letter and requests that you be contacted for an interview. You may mention here that your references are available upon request.

8. The closing ("Sincerely," or "Yours truly," followed by your signature with your name typed under it).

Your cover letter, including all of the information above, should be no more than one page in length. The language used should be polite, businesslike, and to the point. Do not attempt to tell your life story in the cover letter. A long and cluttered letter will only serve to put off the reader. Remember, you need to mention only a few of your accomplishments and skills in the cover letter. The rest of your information is in the resume. If your cover letter is a success, your resume will be read and all pertinent information reviewed by your prospective employer.

Producing the Cover Letter

Cover letters should always be individualized, since they are always written to particular individuals and companies. Never use a form letter for your cover letter. Each one should be as personal as possible. Of course, once you have written and rewritten your first cover letter until you are satisfied with it, you can certainly use similar wording in subsequent letters.

After you have typed your cover letter on quality bond paper, proofread it as thoroughly as you did your resume. Again, spelling errors are a sure sign of carelessness, and you don't want that to be a part of the first impression you give a prospective employer. Handle the letter and resume carefully to avoid any smudges, and then mail both your cover letter and resume in an appropriately sized envelope. Keep an accurate record of all the resumes you send out and the results of each mailing.

Numerous sample cover letters appear at the end of this book. Use them as models for your own cover letter or to get an idea of how cover letters are put together. Remember, every cover letter is unique and depends on the particular circumstances of the individual writing it and the job for which he or she is applying.

About a week after mailing resumes and covers letters to potential employers, contact them by telephone. Confirm that your resume arrived, and ask whether an interview is possible. This makes you appear organized and genuinely interested in the position for which you are applying. Getting your foot in the door during this call is an important part of landing a job, and a strong resume and cover letter will help you immeasurably.

Chapter 5

Sample Resumes

This chapter contains dozens of sample resumes for people pursuing a wide variety of jobs and careers after their military service. There are many different styles of resumes in terms of graphic layout and presentation of information. These samples also represent people with varying amounts of education and work experience. Model your resume after these samples. Choose one resume or borrow elements from several different resumes to help you construct your own.

DARYL S. KAUFMAN

303 Fairfax Avenue
Charleston, WV 25302
(304) 555-4685 (voice)
(304) 555-4695 (fax)

PROFESSIONAL OBJECTIVE

Challenging position as a caseworker or counselor

EDUCATION

Associate in Applied Science
Marshall University, 1998
Huntington, WV
Major: Social Work

Completed additional training at Naval Drug Rehabilitation Center, San Diego, CA

EXPERIENCE

U.S. Navy 1998 - 2002. Served in a counseling capacity, specializing in drug and alcohol counseling.

Marshall University, Huntington, WV, 2002 - present. Part-time counseling assistant, assigned to student health center.

SPECIAL SKILLS/COMPETENCIES

• Adept at working with people

• Experienced in counseling persons with various problems/needs

• Skilled in interviewing techniques, administration and scoring of psychological tests, and other counseling strategies

• Experienced in screening and evaluating persons with substance abuse problems and assisting in managing substance abuse programs

REFERENCES ARE AVAILABLE ON REQUEST.

JAMES P. WODYNSKI
212 Harding Avenue
Evanston, IL 60201
(312) 555-2530
E-mail at: jwody@xxx.net

EXPERIENCE

Enlisted Personnel, United States Coast Guard
Ratings held: Progressed from Seaman Recruit (E-l) to Radarman First Class (E-6)
Active Service: 1995–2003
Reserve Duty: Present
Duties: Operated radar and associated equipment

Representative tasks completed:

- Collected, processed, displayed, evaluated, and disseminated information related to movement of ships, aircraft, and other objects
- Performed duties related to navigation and piloting
- Prepared and maintained records and logs for Combat Information Center operations and operating equipment
- Understood and used Nautical Rules of the Road
- Prepared requisitions for supplies
- Computed statistics necessary for operational reports
- Prepared preventive maintenance schedules

EDUCATIONAL BACKGROUND

Graduate, Yorktown Training Center, VA
Successfully completed additional Coast Guard courses including Radioman First Class (Course No. 139-5) via Coast Guard Institute, Oklahoma City, OK

SPECIAL SKILLS

Excellent quantitative skills
Adept at use of various computer software

REFERENCES PROVIDED ON REQUEST

CARLETTA A. WILLIAMS

2821 Crown Drive
Conway, South Carolina 29526
(803) 555-2833

SUMMARY OF EXPERIENCE

- Twelve years of experience in the United States Army.
- Progressed to rank of Warrant Officer.
- Specialized in maintaining and operating field artillery radars to provide target location.

TECHNICAL AREAS OF EXPERTISE

- Knowledge of effective practices in management and supervision.
- Knowledge of operational aspects of field artillery.
- Close familiarity with technical principles of equipment construction.
- Understanding of safety applications relevant to operations and maintenance.
- Solid understanding of basic electronics theory.

EMPLOYMENT HISTORY

U.S Army, 1990–2002.

Position: Target Acquisition Radar Technician

Served with distinction including postings at the following:

    Fort Knox, Kentucky
    Fort Sill, Oklahoma
    Operation Desert Storm (Persian Gulf)
    Fort Jackson, South Carolina

Rank: Warrant Officer

Awards: Received several medals and commendations. Listing and complete military record available on request.

EDUCATION

Associate Degree, Jefferson Community College, Louisville, Kentucky, 1993 (general studies). Graduate, Army Field Artillery School, 1994.

MEMBERSHIPS

Member, Women's Leadership Association

REFERENCES

Available on request.

ROBERT WILCOX

1805 Grayland Avenue
Price, UT 84501
(801) 555-1918 home phone
(801) 555-9089 cell phone

EMPLOYMENT OBJECTIVE

Position in the telephone, power, or cable industry

RELATED EXPERIENCE

Line Installer and Repairer, U.S. Navy, 1996–2002
Performed a variety of duties involved in installing, maintaining, and repairing electrical cables and communication lines, including:

- Utility pole erection
- Mechanical lift, plow, and other equipment operation
- Overhead communications and electrical cable installation between utility poles
- Installation of street lights and other lighting systems
- Splicing and sealing cables for watertightness
- Installation of voltage regulators, electrical transformers, and voltage regulators
- Related duties

EDUCATION

Completed special training including program in cable splicing and repair at Navy Construction Training Center, Port Hueneme, CA, 1996

REFERENCES AVAILABLE ON REQUEST

LYNN VALENTINE
1218 Grove Avenue
Marquette, MI 49855
(906) 555-8228

Career Objective: Position in Optical Technology or related area.

Occupational Accomplishments

Served in the United States Army as an Optical Laboratory Specialist. In this capacity, performed duties including the following:

- Made and duplicated prescription lenses
- Performed various tasks such as selecting proper stock to fulfill requirements, computing and recording curvature and thickness, edging lenses to correct size and shape, selecting and assembling lens frame components, mounting lenses and aligning frames, completing various calculations
- Maintained records of prescriptions and inventory of supplies and equipment
- Supervised junior personnel
- Assigned duties and trained subordinates
- Supervised quality control procedures
- Completed administrative reports
- Earned outstanding performance ratings

Military Service Record

Active Duty, 1996–2003.
U.S. Army Reserve, Present.
Received several awards and commendations. Complete service record available.

Educational Background

Associate Degree, Midlands Technical College, Columbia, SC, 1999.
Grade point average: 3.5 (4-point scale)
Additional specialized training in Army courses included optical laboratory procedures, information management, personnel supervision, and organizational management.

References Available

HARRISON TILLMAN
420 Reagan Road
Fort Smith, AR 72913
(501) 555-0409

EXPERIENCE

Pharmacy Specialist, United States Army, 1996 - 2002.

Clerk, Goodson's Drugs, Little Rock, AR 1994 - 1996 (part-time).

EDUCATION

B.S. in progress. University of Arkansas (degree anticipated 2003).

Graduate, Medical Field Service School, Fort Sam Houston, TX, 1997.

Successfully completed 715-hour training program in providing auxiliary pharmacy services.

Diploma, George Washington High School, Little Rock, AR, 1996. Honor roll student.

PROFESSIONAL SKILLS

- Highly experienced in providing support to pharmacists and physicians by preparing, controlling, and issuing pharmaceutical products.
- Assisted pharmacists in performing a wide range of duties.
- Compounded and filled prescription orders.
- Performed storage, accounting, inventory, and control procedures.
- Issued medications under pharmacists' supervision.
- Assisted in pharmacy inspections.
- Maintained stock levels and ordered supplies.
- Performed other related duties.

RECOGNITIONS

Earned several awards including Army Good Conduct Medal and Superior Unit Award.

Received excellent evaluations from superiors.

REFERENCES

Available on request.

DONALD P. SPOONER
88 Meadowview Townhomes
Fort Lauderdale, Florida 33301
(305) 555-1692 home
(305) 555-5467 cellular

CAREER OBJECTIVE

To obtain a position in the construction industry utilizing skills and experienced gained as an experienced carpenter

EDUCATION

Graduate, U.S. Army Engineer School, Fort Leonard Wood, Missouri (eight-week training course in carpentry/masonry)

High school diploma with vocational training in construction, Wilson High School, Fort Lauderdale, Florida

RELATED EXPERIENCE

- Fabricated, erected, and maintained/repaired wooden and masonry structures on U.S. Army bases
- Attained advanced skill level and provided technical guidance and supervision of other personnel
- Performed complex construction activities including interpreting blueprints, estimating material needs, and installing finished carpentry product
- Mastered use of a variety of tools including power tools
- Performed a comprehensive array of tasks including erection of building components such as floors, roofing systems, walls, and stairs
- Completed both rough and finish work while working in a timely fashion

REFERENCES PROVIDED ON REQUEST

MICHAEL SHEPPARD

1056 King Street Extension

Huntington, IN 46750

(219) 555-8465 home phone

(219) 555-3657 cellular phone

PROFESSIONAL EXPERIENCE

Seven years' experience in the United States Army (1996 - 2003), specializing as a parachute rigger

JOB DUTIES

- Packed both aircraft cargo and personnel parachutes
- Fabricated, assembled, and rigged airdrop equipment
- Loaded, positioned, and secured cargo for airdrop
- Inspected and inventoried airdrop equipment
- Provided technical guidance to less experienced personnel
- Tested ripcord and canopy release assemblies
- Conducted inspections of airdrop equipment

EDUCATION

Graduate, Quartermaster School, Ft. Lee, VA (396-hour course in advanced parachute rigging), 1997

Graduate, Jefferson High School, Huntington, IN, 1996

REFERENCES

Available on request

DAVID C. SCHULZ
1308 Ellis Road
Glendale, AZ 85306
(602) 555-5121 home phone
(602) 555-5673 cellular phone

OBJECTIVE: A position in financial management, warehousing, logistics management, purchasing, or a related field

RELEVANT SKILLS AND EXPERIENCE

Fifteen years' experience in the United States Coast Guard, specializing in finance and supply (1988 - 2003). At time of retirement, had progressed to rank of Warrant Officer.

- Served as a technical specialist in finance and supply
- Planned, organized, and supervised the work of storekeepers, subsistence specialists, and other finance and supply personnel
- Supervised the inventory of supplies and equipment
- Planned and supervised the preparation of budgets, payrolls, and other information
- Coordinated preparation for regular audits
- Directed the organization and upkeep of department records

SPECIAL TRAINING

Military courses, seminars, and college courses completed in these areas:

- accounting systems
- principles of management
- technical communications
- logistics management
- personnel supervision
- fundamentals of purchasing and supply
- budget processes

REFERENCES ON REQUEST

JUAN SANCHEZ

3838 16th Street
San Bernardino, CA 92401
(714) 555-6155

OBJECTIVE

Responsible position requiring proven mechanical skills.

ACHIEVEMENTS

• Provided comprehensive mechanical services for military aircraft.

• Received excellent evaluations from superiors.

• Earned three promotions in rank based on job accomplishments and overall performance.

WORK EXPERIENCE

United States Coast Guard, 1996–2002
Specialty: Aircraft maintenance and repair
Rating: Aviation Structural Mechanic First Class (E-6)
Responsibilities:
• Performed comprehensive duties related to handling, inspecting, servicing, and maintaining aircraft structures and components.

• Fabricated and assembled metal parts.

• Made repairs.

• Performed nondestructive testing.

• Painted and maintained painting equipment.

• Maintained hydraulic systems, landing gear, fuel tanks, and other components.

• Performed related duties.

EDUCATION

Graduate, Aviation Training Technical Center, USCG, Elizabeth City, North Carolina, 1997

Diploma, Warren High School, San Bernardino, California, 1996

REFERENCES

Available on request

TYRONE H. ROBERTS

17 N. Franklin St.
Valencia, CA 91355
(805) 555-5145

EMPLOYMENT OBJECTIVE

To obtain a position involving installation or repair of electrical systems and components

CAREER HISTORY

Ten years' outstanding service maintaining and repairing aircraft electrical systems in the United States Marine Corps

Honorably discharged at rank of sergeant (E-5) after service as Aircraft Electrical Systems Technician, 2002

WORK BACKGROUND

Installed and repaired electrical components and systems on military aircraft

Inspected and tested electrical components

Diagnosed equipment malfunctions

Demonstrated thorough working knowledge of diodes, transistors, integrated circuits, motors, and other electrical components

Performed Level 3 tasks including conducting pre-flight and post-flight operational tests on electrical systems

REFERENCES WILL BE PROVIDED ON REQUEST

DENNIS R. RILEY

606 Tall Oaks Lane
Helena, MT 59624
(406) 555-6540

CAREER OBJECTIVE

Position as a civilian pilot or in a management/support role within the aviation industry

EDUCATION

B.S. United States Air Force Academy, 1990
Graduated in top 20 percent of class
M.S. in Management, Georgetown University, Washington, DC, 1998

MILITARY EXPERIENCE

- Highly experienced as accomplished pilot on active duty with the U.S. Air Force (1990–2003)
- Experienced in flying a variety of aircraft, with emphasis on the F-16, and comprehensive training as a combat pilot
- Active participant in Operation Desert Storm with several medals/citations (complete list available)
- Highly skilled in all aspects of aircraft operation
- Exemplary military record with option to continue in service still available at time of leaving military

SPECIAL KNOWLEDGE & SKILLS

Outstanding analytical skills
Highly flexible in taking on new assignments
Diligent in applying sound safety skills to all aspects of aviation practice and management

MEMBERSHIPS

Aviation Society of America
Rotary International

REFERENCES AVAILABLE ON REQUEST

COLLEEN QUINN
3104 Linden Court
Bradford, MA 01830
(508) 555-9576 home
(508) 555-0909 cellular
E-mail: cquinn@xxx.net

CAREER OBJECTIVE: A position in computer repair, installation, or service

PROFESSIONAL EXPERIENCE

- Served in U.S. Army, 1993–2003. Specialized in servicing and repairing computer systems supporting advanced communications equipment
- Performed a wide range of tasks in servicing, installing, and repairing computers and related equipment
- Installed computers and computer systems
- Diagnosed equipment problems and identified equipment malfunctions
- Installed printers and other peripheral devices
- Serviced and replaced components of computers and related equipment
- Transported computer equipment to and from repair locations, as well as performing work on-site
- Maintained up-to-date knowledge of advancements in computer technology

MILITARY SERVICE BACKGROUND

Reached rank of Sergeant

Earned excellent performance evaluations

EDUCATION

Successfully completed 1,036-hour training course in Automated Computer Systems Repair at Fort Gordon, Georgia

Completed 30 semester hours in computer technology, electronics, and related subjects at Aiken Technical College, Aiken, South Carolina, and Jefferson Community College, Lexington, Kentucky

Completed additional correspondence courses and other Army training courses

References, including complete military records, are available upon request.

RASHEED B. SMITH II
11 Hillcrest Drive • Columbia, SC 29202
(803) 555-1859

EXPERIENCE

1999 - 2002   **Equal Opportunity Program Specialist, U.S. Navy (E-7)**
Classification: Chief Petty Officer
Duties: Served as advisor to officers on equal opportunity matters, provided training in non-discrimination practices, assisted in formulating and revising equal opportunity directives, performed related duties.

1994 - 1999   **Personnelman, U.S. Navy (E-6)**
Classification: Advanced from Personnelman Third Class to Personnelman First Class
Duties: Provided a variety of personel administration duties.

1993 - 1994   **Seaman, U.S. Navy (E-3)**
Duties: Performed basic seamanship functions.

EDUCATION

B.S., University of South Carolina, 1998
Major: Political Science
Minor: Sociology

Graduate, Defense Equal Opportunity Training Institute, 1997

Completed Navy Instructor Training Program, 1997

REFERENCES

Available on request.

JASON RASKIN

1005 University Blvd.
Fort Collins, CO 80523
(303) 555-6922

CAREER OBJECTIVE

To obtain a position in auto body repair

RELATED EXPERIENCE

Experienced in repairing frames and bodies of trucks, automobiles, and other vehicles

Skilled in using a wide range of tools and equipment

Experienced in tasks such as
     Replacing damaged body parts
     Straightening frames, doors, hoods, and fenders
     Welding damaged frames and auto body parts
     Installing glass windows
     Refinishing body surfaces
     Completing other related tasks

WORK BACKGROUND

Served in United States Army, 1996–2003
     Specialized in providing auto body repair services for Army vehicles
     Worked well with diverse personnel

Webb Auto Repair, 1994–1996 (part-time and summers)

Fort Collins, CO
     Provided general services ranging from cleanup to assisting in basic auto body repair functions; range of duties progressed during job tenure

TRAINING

Completed certificate in auto body repair, Rocky Mountain Technical College, 1995

Completed additional training through military courses

REFERENCES PROVIDED ON REQUEST

ROBERTO A. REYES

1378 Orchard Street NE

Santa Fe, NM 87501

(505) 555-4056

WORK EXPERIENCE

1998 - present. Infantry Senior Sergeant, U.S. Army
Serving as principal operations officer of an infantry brigade.

1995 - 1998. Infantryman, U.S. Army
Performed basic functions necessary as a member of a highly trained
combat brigade.

1994 - 1995. Store clerk, J-Mart Corporation, Santa Fe, NM
Stocked merchandise and checked out customers.

EDUCATION

Diploma, Anderson High School, Santa Fe, NM. Graduated June 1994.

Completed several Army training courses, 1995 - 2001.

SPECIAL SKILLS

- Experienced, proven leader.
- Provided day-to-day leadership to enlisted personnel in carrying out complex, highly difficult assignments requiring both physical fitness and problem-solving capabilities.
- Earned commendations for leadership, marksmanship, and other job performance factors.

REFERENCES

Provided on request.

RICARDO SMITH
15 Orchard Court Drive
Baltimore, Maryland 21202
Home: (301) 555-1218
Cellular: (301) 555-9087

SUMMARY OF QUALIFICATIONS

Experienced and highly competent dental hygienist.
Adept at interacting with people and creating a nonthreatening environment.

ACCOMPLISHMENTS

Served successfully on active duty with the United States Navy as a dental hygienist. Received outstanding performance evaluations. Helped unit earn citation for excellence, 2000 and 2001. Served in volunteer capacity through special program providing dental care for disadvantaged children, 2001 - 2002.

EMPLOYMENT HISTORY

1993 - 2002 Dental Hygienist, United States Navy.
Rank: Petty Officer First Class
Locations of service:

> U.S. Naval Station, Agana, Guam, 2001 - 2002

> Naval Medical Command, Bethesda, MD, 1993 - 2001

EDUCATION

Associate in science degree (Dental Hygiene), 1993
Towson State University
Baltimore, MD 21204
GPA: 3.75 (4.0 scale)
Member, student government

CERTIFICATES/LICENSES

Certified, National Dental Hygiene Board
Certified, Mid-Atlantic Regional Dental Hygiene Board

MEMBERSHIPS

Member, American Dental Hygiene Association
Member, Maryland Dental Hygiene Society
Member, Local United Way Advisory Committee

REFERENCES

Provided on request

STUART PURDY, JR.

Route 4, Box 189
Winfield, KS 67156
(316) 555-0370 home
(316) 555-9676 cellular

EMPLOYMENT HISTORY:

2000–2003 Recruiter, U.S. Army

1994–2000 Infantryman, U.S. Army

1992–1994 Sales Associate, Wilson Insurance Company, Winfield, KS

EXPERIENCE SUMMARY:

- As Army recruiter, contacted and interviewed individuals as potential enlistees
- Contacted representatives of schools and coordinated recruiting visits
- Presented formal and informal talks to various groups
- Distributed publicity materials
- Conducted market research and analysis

EDUCATION:

Graduate, Recruiting and Retention School, Ft. Benjamin Harrison, IN, 2000

MEMBERSHIPS:

Member, Toastmasters International

REFERENCES:

Available on Request

LOUISE PRUETTE

Route 2, Box 21A

Jackson Heights, MS 39212

(601) 555-1574 (voice)

(601) 555-1145 (fax)

POSITION DESIRED

Responsible position in business management

WORK EXPERIENCE

U.S. Army, 1997–2002
Rank: Captain
Specialty: Armament Material Management
Duties:

- Managed logistical functions.

- Supervised warehouse and transportation personnel.

- Performed planning, quality assurance, evaluation, and related duties as part of Army support unit providing munitions and supplies.

EDUCATION

Bachelor of Business Administration, Radford University, Radford, VA, 1997.

Also successfully completed Army R.O.T.C. program.

Member, Alpha Kappa Tau Business Honor Society.

Master of Business Administration, Clemson University, Clemson, SC, 2001.

MEMBERSHIPS

Member, U.S. Army Reserve

Member, American Logistics Management Association

REFERENCES

Provided on request

DONALD E. PFEIFER

3188 Bradshaw Road
Manchester, CT 06040
(203) 555-1286 home office
(203) 555-8787 cellular

EMPLOYMENT OBJECTIVE

To obtain a position in graphic design or related area requiring advanced design and illustration skills

RELATED SKILLS AND EXPERIENCE

- Highly experienced in graphic design and illustration
- Experienced in various techniques for developing illustrations for posters, graphs, charts, training aids, brochures, books, and other publications
- Accomplished in using a variety of media including pencil, pen and ink, water color, art markers, and other media
- Skilled in producing both realistic and cartoon-style drawings and other illustrations
- Experienced in using a wide range of equipment including copy cameras, orthographic equipment, and other graphics arts and audiovisual presentation equipment
- Highly flexible in completing different types of assignments, working with others, and using creativity in practical applications

WORK BACKGROUND

1994–2002 Chief Illustrator Draftsman (E-7), United States Navy.
Honorably discharged after nine years of service; decided against re-enlistment in favor of civilian life. Received several promotions and recognitions; complete military record available on request. Portfolio also available.

REFERENCES WILL BE PROVIDED ON REQUEST

PAULA L. PATTERSON, M.D.

2311 Lawrence Street
Emmitsburg, MD 21727
(301) 555-6122

OBJECTIVE: A POSITION IN MEDICAL RESEARCH

EDUCATION

M.D., University of Virginia Medical School, 1996.

M.S., University of Virginia, Charlottesville, VA, 1992.
Biology
4.0 grade point average

B.S., Virginia Tech, Blacksburg, VA, 1991.
Major: Chemistry
Minor: Biology
3.9 (4.0 scale) grade point average

PROFESSIONAL EXPERIENCE

Active Duty, U.S. Navy, 1996–2002.

Assignment: Research Scientist, Naval Medical Research and
Development Command, Bethesda, MD

Duties: Conducted research on new approaches to combat casualty care

Research interest: Preservation of blood components and substitutes;
development of blood component substitutes

Accomplishments: Made substantial progress in developing new, effective
blood component substitutes

PUBLICATIONS

Articles in over ten publications including several in *Cell, Hematology,* and
other refereed journals. Complete list available.

Page one of two

Dr. Paula L. Patterson - Page two of two

AWARDS/RECOGNITIONS

Outstanding Science Student, Virginia Tech class of 1984 (one of only three graduates to receive this award)

Graduated *summa cum laude* from Virginia Tech

Received Rawlings Fellowship, University of Virginia

"Outstanding Young Woman of America," 1998

Received several Navy awards along with excellent evaluations

VOLUNTEERISM

Active in "Big Sister" program, Bethesda, MD

Volunteer, Special Olympics, Blacksburg, VA

REFERENCES ON REQUEST

ROBERT C. PEREZ

Apartment 4-B, Anderson Ridge Apartments
3400 Bryant Avenue
Worcester, MA 01608
(508) 555-1486

Career Objective

A position where I can use my mechanical skills and aptitudes.

Occupational Accomplishments

Served in the United States Navy as a Boiler Technician.
Operated and performed maintenance on boilers, pumps, and related machinery.
Advanced to Boiler Technician First Class.
Developed a wide range of mechanical and operational skills.

Military Service Record

Active Duty, 1995–2001
Served aboard U.S.S. *John C. Stennis*

U.S. Navy Reserve, 2001–Present
Complete service record available on request

Educational Background

Graduate, Service School Command, Great Lakes, IL.

Completed courses on performing preventive and corrective maintenance on steam propulsion systems and components.

References

Provided on request.

ROGER E. NUNN

707 Washington Terrace
Concord, NH 03301
(603) 555-2152

CAREER OBJECTIVE

To obtain a position in machining, machine tool technology, or related field.

EDUCATION

A.S. degree, New Hampshire Vocational-Technical College, Manchester, NH, 1990. Emphasis area: machine tool technology.

Additional education through U.S. Army training courses. Subjects covered included personnel supervision, records management, and organizational management.

RELATED EXPERIENCE

Allied Trades Technician, U.S. Army, 1997 - 2003.

Machinist, U.S. Army, 1989 - 1997.

Rank at end of Army service: Chief Warrant Officer

- Set up and operated machine tools
- Made and repaired metal parts, mechanisms, and machinery
- Supervised subordinates in setting up and using equipment
- Managed shop operations
- Interpreted regulations and orders
- Performed comprehensive duties requiring firsthand knowledge of metalworking techniques and practices, as well as effective supervisory techniques

SPECIAL ACCOMPLISHMENTS

Contributed to several issues of Preventive Maintenance Monthly, *1994 - 1998.*

Selected to serve on special review team for revision of technical manuals, 1999.

REFERENCES PROVIDED ON REQUEST

Allen P. Olessi

21 Ball Terrace
Spartanburg, SC 29303
(803) 555-4088

SUMMARY OF QUALIFICATIONS

Highly skilled manager experienced in providing leadership for complex, demanding operations. Experienced through service as officer in United States Navy in various aspects of planning, managing, motivating, evaluating, and implementing action plans. Decisive, energetic supervisor.

ACCOMPLISHMENTS

Recently completed a highly successful twenty-year career with the United States Navy. Served in several highly important roles, including Executive Officer of an aircraft carrier with a crew of more than 5,000.

PROFESSIONAL EXPERIENCE

U.S. Navy, 1982–2002.
Began career as an Ensign assigned to U.S.S. *Tarawa*. Also served on U.S.S. *Virginia*, U.S.S. *Forrestal,* and U.S.S. *Nimitz*, where I served as Executive Officer. Reached rank of Commander. Received numerous commendations and recognitions for service. Complete military record available on request.

EDUCATION

M.S. in Management, Virginia State University, Petersburg, VA, 1992.

B.S., Georgia Institute of Technology, Atlanta, GA, 1982.
Major: Business Administration
Minor: Military Science (member, Naval R.O.T.C.)
GPA: 3.4

Additional training obtained through various Navy courses.

REFERENCES PROVIDED ON REQUEST

H. BRIAN PAINTER

507 Sunnyview Place
Boulder, CO 80306
(303) 555-4557

CAREER OBJECTIVE

To obtain a position requiring excellent organizational and leadership skills

MILITARY SERVICE/PROFESSIONAL EXPERIENCE

2001–2003 Fleet Marine Force, Atlantic. Norfolk, Virginia.
        Rank: Captain

1994–2001 First Marine Amphibious Force. Camp Pendleton, California.
        Rank: First Lieutenant (promoted from Second Lieutenant 1997)

1990–1994 Student member, Reserve Officer Training Corps (ROTC), University of
        Colorado. Boulder, Colorado.

DUTIES/SKILLS

In all positions as Marine Corps officer, provided key role in training, preparing, and leading combat-ready troops.

Specialized in amphibious operations. Duties required assertiveness, mental and physical vigor, highly developed leadership qualities, loyalty, and excellent skills in planning, organizing, and managing.

EDUCATION

Bachelor of Science, University of Colorado, 1994.
Major: Business Management
Minor: Marketing
24 credits toward master's degree, Old Dominion University, Norfolk, Virginia

REFERENCES PROVIDED ON REQUEST

CHRISTOPHER PASCOE

PERMANENT ADDRESS:
21 Lake Avenue Circle
Palos Heights, Illinois 60463
(312) 555-4376 (voice)
(312) 555-6062 (fax)

SUMMARY OF QUALIFICATIONS

Experienced, highly competent plumber and pipefitter. Developed and applied plumbing skills while on active duty in United States Army. Reliable worker. Skilled at working productively and efficiently.

WORK EXPERIENCE

Plumber, United States Army, 1987 - 2002.

Duties: Performed basic plumbing services, including installation and maintenance

Rank: Sergeant

Performance level: Received various service awards and recognitions (complete military record available)

Laborer, United Cities Construction, Palos Heights, Illinois (summers, 1985 - 1986)

EDUCATION

Graduate, Engineer School, Fort Leonard Wood, Missouri, 1987 (Plumbing Course 720-51KIO)

REFERENCES

Available on request

MARVIN MAHAFFEY

2144 Falconer Highway

Louisville, KY 40232

(502) 555-0496

SUMMARY OF QUALIFICATIONS

Expert, experienced technician trained in maintaining, servicing, and repairing radio equipment

PROFESSIONAL EXPERIENCE

1995–2003 United States Navy

Position: Electronics Technician First Class

Specialty: Radio equipment maintenance and repair

Responsibilities: Performed comprehensive services in installing, maintaining, and repairing radio equipment. Read and interpreted schematics. Used a variety of tools and equipment. Performed troubleshooting functions. Prepared preventive maintenance schedules. Maintained parts inventory. Provided other related duties.

EDUCATION/TRAINING

Graduate, Service School Command, San Diego, CA, 1996.

Completed Navy training courses in basic electronics, AC and DC circuits, electronic instrumentation, radio set maintenance, and related subjects.

REFERENCES

Reference information provided on request.

MARILYN H. MACAULEY

Until June 1, 2003   After June 1, 2003
910 Collins Street   277 Fairview Extension
Apartment 6B   Portland, ME 04101
Burlington, VT 05401   (207) 555-4404
(802) 555-7137

EDUCATIONAL BACKGROUND

Associate in Applied Science (engineering technology), Trident Technical College, Charleston, South Carolina, 1996.

Twelve semester hours at University of South Carolina (engineering and business).

Naval training courses completed in a variety of areas including:
• basic aircraft maintenance
• aircraft jet engine maintenance
• propeller, fuel, and exhaust systems maintenance
• basic helicopter drive system maintenance
• aircraft maintenance management
• personnel administration

WORK EXPERIENCE

Chief Aviation Machinists' Mate (E-7), U.S. Navy. Left military service voluntarily to return to civilian life, 2002. Stationed at Charleston Naval Base, Charleston, South Carolina.

page one of two

WORK EXPERIENCE (CONTINUED)

Took on increasing levels of responsibility and gained expertise, serving as Airman, Aviation Machinists' Mate, Third Class, Second Class, and First Class.

Mastered comprehensive array of skills involved in maintaining aircraft engines and related systems. Became thoroughly familiar with induction, cooling, fuel, oil, compression, combustion, turbine, and exhaust systems. Conducted a wide range of service and repair tasks.

Performed management role that included supervising work groups and completing tasks related to planning and management.

SPECIAL SKILLS

Highly skilled at performing complex tasks needed to provide safe, efficient service, maintenance, and repair of aircraft.

Experienced in supervising others and managing the planning and execution of maintenance and repair functions.

REFERENCES AVAILABLE ON REQUEST

Michael Melendez
3350 Brookside Avenue
Salem, OR 97309
(503) 555-2381

Objective: A challenging position in the food service industry

---

Education:

A.A.S., Seattle Community College, 1990
Major: Food Service Management

Additional training through U.S. Army

Work Experience:

Served as Food Service Technician, U. S. Army
Rank: Warrant Officer, 1988–2002

Experience: Fifteen years' highly successful performance, receiving consistently high evaluations from superior officers. Performed the following duties:

- Supervised and administered comprehensive food service activities for large military installation

- Maintained operational control over personnel, facilities, and equipment

- Supervised procurement, storage, distribution, and preparation of foods

- Performed wide range of duties with emphasis on technical and human resource areas of food service administration

- Exercised both reliability in carrying out policies and directives and creativity in enhancing various aspects of food preparation, service, and overall management

---

Memberships:

National Food Service Association
Optimists International

References:

Provided on request

SARAH KABULSKI-LONG

1305 Glade Spring Circle
Santa Cruz, CA 95064
(408) 555-3323

EMPLOYMENT OBJECTIVE

To obtain a position in computer support services utilizing my training in computer programming

RELATED SKILLS AND EXPERIENCE

- Experienced in writing, analyzing, testing, and implementing computer programs
- Competent in COBOL, C++, BASIC, Pascal, and World Wide Web page design, setup, and maintenance
- Experienced in conducting data systems studies involving investigation, evaluation, development, and implementation of new and modified data processing systems
- Skilled in applying advanced programming techniques

WORK BACKGROUND

Programmer/Analyst, United States Army, 1999–2002

Computer/Machine Operator, United States Army, 1995–1999

TRAINING/EDUCATION

Bachelor of Science, University of the Pacific, 2003.
Major: Computer Science
Minor: Mathematics

Completed Army training courses at Information Systems Software Center, Fort Belvoir, Virginia.

REFERENCES WILL BE PROVIDED ON REQUEST

SUSAN A. LOMBARDO

PERMANENT ADDRESS:
21 Lake Avenue Circle
Palos Heights, Illinois 60463
(312) 555-4376 (voice)
(312) 555-6062 (fax)

SUMMARY OF QUALIFICATIONS

• Experienced military police officer.

• Highly trained and experienced in performing basic law enforcement duties.

• Dependable, levelheaded, and energetic.

• Adept at using good judgment in a wide range of settings and situations.

WORK EXPERIENCE

United States Army, 1995–2003

Role: Military Police Officer

Duties: Performed a wide range of duties. Experience included base security, routine and special patrols, traffic management, and assisting in criminal investigations.

EDUCATION

Graduate of Military Police School, Fort McClellan, Alabama.

Completed additional courses in criminal investigation methods, Fort Gordon, Georgia.

High school graduate with six college credits through dual enrollment program (English Composition and American History).

TECHNICAL SKILLS

Highly skilled in a wide range of law enforcement skills including crowd control, appropriate weapons use, and arrest procedures.

REFERENCES
Personal and professional references available on request.

CARTER KATZ
474 East Triangle Street
Adrian, MI 49221
(517) 555-2686

CAREER OBJECTIVE: A position in mailroom management or related field

---

EXPERIENCE

Postal Specialist, United States Army, 2000–2003

- Performed a variety of duties involved in processing domestic and international mail.
- Requisitioned, safeguarded, and issued stamps, money orders, supplies, and equipment.
- Maintained and audited postal accounts.
- Operated and supervised postal service center and integrated retail terminals.

Package Handler, United Parcel Service, 1999–2000

Loaded and unloaded trucks; performed miscellaneous duties as part-time, temporary employee.

EDUCATION AND TRAINING

Completed Postal Supervisor Course, Soldier Support Center, Fort Benjamin Harrison, IN, 2000

Additional studies completed through correspondence and other Army training in personnel management and accounting.

Diploma, South High School, Minneapolis, MN

SPECIAL SKILLS/KNOWLEDGE

Familiar with a variety of equipment including

- manual and automated postage meters
- postage scales
- electronic mail sorting equipment
- bar code printers and readers

REFERENCES AVAILABLE ON REQUEST

JUDY L. CHANG

Apartment 19, Greenacre Estates
500 South Parkway
Muncie, Indiana 47306
(317) 555-3316 (home)
(317) 555-9745 (cellular)

OBJECTIVE

A position in secretarial support, administration, or marketing.

EXPERIENCE

1998 - 2003   Administrative Specialist, United States Army.
- Served as executive administrative assistant.
- Typed and word-processed documents.
- Prepared correspondence and reports.
- Filed records and coordinated filing systems.
- Provided general administrative support.
- Promoted from administrative clerk, providing basic office support functions.

EDUCATION

Graduate, Adjutant General School, Soldier Support Institute.
Fort Benjamin Harrison, Indiana, 2000.

Completed Administrative Specialist course (self-paced).
Administration School, Fort Jackson, South Carolina.

Six credits in Secretarial Science, 1997.
Indiana Vocational-Technical College, Indianapolis, Indiana.

REFERENCES

Available on request

LATASHA HUGHES JONES

2120 Fairview Avenue
Columbus, OH 43216
(614) 555-1508

CAREER GOAL

A position in emergency services, comprehensive health care, or other health care service.

EXPERIENCE

Six years of active service in the United States Navy (1996–2002). Served most recently as Hospital Corpsman First Class.

ASSIGNMENTS

Meridian Naval Air Station, Meridian, Mississippi

Guantanamo Bay Naval Station, Cuba

PROFESSIONAL SPECIALTY

Emergency services

EDUCATION

A.D.N. Cuyahoga Community College, Cleveland, Ohio, 1996.

Completed additional United States Navy training in records and information management, personnel supervision, and facilities management (Great Lakes Naval Training Center).

MEMBERSHIPS

American Nursing Association

REFERENCES AVAILABLE ON REQUEST

JAMAAL V. JOHNSON
4900 Ridgeway Place
El Paso, TX 79968
(401) 555-1895 Home
(401) 555-6564 Cellular

PROFESSIONAL OBJECTIVE

Seeking a position in the civilian health care field utilizing my skills and experience in physical therapy.

EXPERIENCE

1993–2003 Physical Therapy Specialist, United States Army

Rank: Staff Sergeant

- Performed comprehensive duties in physical therapy treatment and exercises.
- Utilized various techniques including heat, ice, ultrasound, hydrotherapy, massage, electrical stimulation, and manual exercise procedures.
- Prepared patient and administrative reports.
- Assisted in clinic management.

EDUCATION

Graduate, Academy of Health Sciences, Fort Sam Houston, TX, 1993.

Completed both Phase I (17 weeks) and Phase II (10 weeks) in physical therapy techniques.

Completed additional continuing education courses, 1996 and 2000.

REFERENCES

References available on request.

SHAWNA A. JEFFERSON
238 Heather Avenue
Sioux City, Iowa 51104
(712) 555-0960 Home
(712) 555-7430 Cellular

Career Objective

A position providing paralegal assistance in a progressive law practice

Achievements and Experience

Served as a Senior Chief Legalman (E-8) in the United States Navy, 1994–2003. In this capacity, performed the following:

- Fulfilled a wide range of paralegal duties under the supervision of legal officers
- Assisted in preparing legal research using references including federal and state codes, legal encyclopedias, legal digests, and on-line resources
- Coordinated office functions in judge advocate's office
- Reviewed records and reports for accuracy and legal adequacy
- Prepared records and documents using computers, stenotype machines, and other office equipment
- Assisted personnel in obtaining legal services
- Earned outstanding performance ratings

Education

Associate of Arts, Miami-Dade Community College, Miami, Florida, 1992
Graduate, Naval Justice School, Newport, Rhode Island, 1994

Memberships

Member, American Paralegal Society
Member, Civitans

References

Available on request

DENISE JACKSON-SMITH

906 Fair Meadow Townhomes
Dayton, OH 45469
(513) 555-9765

EMPLOYMENT OBJECTIVE

Desire a position in maintaining, servicing, and repairing medical equipment

PROFESSIONAL EXPERIENCE

1994–2002 United States Army
Position: Medical Equipment Repairer, Unit Level

Responsibilities: Provided a wide range of service and repairs for a variety of medical equipment, including the following types:

- mechanical
- electronic
- hydraulic
- digital
- gas
- solid-state
- steam
- radiological
- electrical
- optical

Duties included the following:

- Performed routine maintenance, service, calibration, and repair of medical equipment
- Inspected, inventoried, and assembled new equipment
- Serviced and repaired equipment including pulmonary equipment, monitoring systems, diathermy systems, spectrophotometers, ultrasonic equipment, anesthesia apparatus, operating tables, and other systems and individual units

TRAINING

Completed Army training courses in solid-state electronics, AC circuits, DC circuits, electronic instrumentation, pneumatic and hydraulic controls, mechanical and electromechanical controls, electronic equipment diagnostics and repair, and related subjects.

REFERENCES

Complete reference information will be made available on request.

CHARLES H. INGRAM
Route 4, Box 112
Isleboro, Maine 04848
(207) 555-1219

SUMMARY OF QUALIFICATIONS

Energetic, highly motivated team player experienced in working with others to achieve common goals. Physically fit and mentally vigorous. Available to take on new challenges following successful period of military service.

EXPERIENCE

1997 - 2003 United States Navy
Rating: Mineman First Class (E-6)

- Maintained, installed, and inspected underwater explosive devices
- Instructed junior personnel in handling explosives and detonation agents
- Supervised handling, assembling, disassembling, testing, and storage of mines
- Prepared mine cases and other components for assembly
- Used a wide variety of tools and testing devices
- Performed other related duties requiring diligence, concentration, and adherence to safety

1996 - 1997 Stocker, Cook's Grocery, 21 Main Street, Isleboro, Maine. Performed general store duties while employed on part-time basis.

EDUCATION

Diploma, Isleboro High School, Isleboro, Maine, 1997

Graduate, Fleet and Mine Warfare Training Center, Charleston, South Carolina, 1998

REFERENCES

Available on request

RACHEL E. HUAN

275 Rolling Hills Drive
Toms River, New Jersey 08753
(201) 555-6622 home
(201) 555-8890 cellular phone

Objective

A challenging position in the printing industry.

Work Background

1999–2002 Printing and Binding Specialist, U.S. Army.

1997–1999 Infantryman, U.S. Army.

1995–1997 Office Assistant, Hollings Publications, Toms River, New Jersey.

Printing Experience/Skills

Through Army experience and training, became thoroughly proficient in operating offset presses, bindery equipment, and duplication equipment. This included supervising photolithographic activities as well as performing direct printing and binding tasks.

Education

Completed several U.S. Army training courses.

Graduate, Fairview High School, Fairview, New Jersey.

Special Recognitions

Received commendations for outstanding performance, including good conduct medal and excellent evaluations from superiors.

References available on request

DOUGLAS HINES

526 Calhoun Street
Silver City, NM 88062
(505) 555-4448

JOB OBJECTIVE

To obtain a position utilizing my skill and background as a trained researcher.

WORK EXPERIENCE

1996–2002 ***Biological Sciences Assistant,*** United States Army.
Duties: Performed professional-level laboratory and research duties in biological science.
Conducted studies as part of Army research projects. Some projects classified.
Specialized in small animal nervous systems as affected by toxins.

1994–1996 ***Graduate Research Assistant,*** University of New Mexico.
Duties: Performed general laboratory duties under faculty supervision.

SPECIAL SKILLS/INTERESTS

Skilled in use of computers and related applications in research methodologies.
Working knowledge of German.

PUBLICATIONS

Author or coauthor of several publications. Complete list and/or copies of articles available on request.

EDUCATION

B.S., University of New Mexico, 1994.
Major: Biology
Minor: Chemistry
Graduated *magna cum laude*
Member, Alpha Mu Kappa Honorary Science Society
Dean's List eight semesters

M.S. University of New Mexico, 1996.
Major: Biology
Thesis: "Effects of Pesticides on Amphibian Desert Populations"

MEMBERSHIPS

Member, American Biology Association

REFERENCES PROVIDED ON REQUEST

Lisa M. Henry

532 Monitor Drive
Columbus, OH 43215
(614) 555-3987

PROFESSIONAL EXPERIENCE

2000–2002   Photography Warrant Officer, U.S. Navy

1997–2000   Photographer's Mate, U.S. Navy

1995–1997   Darkroom Assistant, Connor Photography, Columbus, OH
(part-time and summers)

EDUCATION

Graduate, Advanced Photography Training Course, School of Photography,
Corry Station, Pensacola, FL, 2000

College courses completed in photography, technical writing, and general
studies (24 credit hours completed toward bachelor's degree), Virginia
Commonwealth University, Richmond, VA

Completed several additional Navy training courses (completion certificates
and/or transcripts available on request)

SPECIAL SKILLS

- photographic lab techniques
- lab supervision
- color photography
- illustrative photography
- aerial photography
- photojournalism
- portraiture

REFERENCES ON REQUEST

Brian Hawkins

108-B North Madison
College Station, Texas 77843
(409) 555-1245

Employment Objective

Position as an air traffic controller or related position in aviation operation or management

---

Experience

- Fifteen years of experience with the U.S. Army (1986–2001), including twelve years of active service as an ATC operator
- Experienced with Visual Flight Rules (VFR), Special Visual Flight Rules (SVFR), and Instrument Flight Rules (IFR)
- Provided radar and nonradar air traffic control services
- Provided flight control for takeoffs, flight, and landings for military and civilian aircraft
- Performed with excellence and reliability

Education

Completed ATC training at Aviation Center, Fort Rucker, Alabama, 1989

Membership

Association of Air Traffic Controllers

References

References and additional background information, including transcripts, are available on request

TAWNYA A. GROVES
3200 Old Farm Road
Kearney, NE 68849
(308) 555-0409
Fax: (308) 555-6618

JOB OBJECTIVE

To obtain a position in inventory, logistics management, or another related field

EDUCATION

University of Maryland, College Park, Maryland.
Completed forty semester hours in business administration.
Completed several special trainings on property accounting/management at Quartermaster School, Fort Lee, VA.

WORK EXPERIENCE

1996–2002: Property Accounting Technician, U.S. Navy.
Rank: Warrant Officer
Duties:
- Performed comprehensive duties related to property accountability.
- Managed property books, both manual and automated.
- Utilized appropriate accounting procedures. Planned supply requirements and completed forecasts.
- Established procedures for obtaining, storing, and issuing supplies.
- Prepared reports and correspondence.
- Completed additional related duties.
- Advanced through promotion from previous position of Unit Supply Specialist.

1994–1996: Child Care Worker, Tots, Inc., Kearney, NE

SPECIAL SKILLS/INTERESTS

- Skilled in use of computers
- Conversant in American Sign Language (ASL)
- Volunteer interpreter for the deaf

MEMBERSHIPS

- American Logistics Association
- Nebraska Interpreters League

REFERENCES PROVIDED ON REQUEST

ALLISON GOSNEY

206 Jeffries Drive
Riverdale, NY 10471
(212) 555-2013

EMPLOYMENT OBJECTIVE

To obtain a challenging position in the airline industry

RELATED SKILLS AND EXPERIENCE

- Experienced in various aspects of providing service for air passengers
- Skilled in all steps required for processing passenger reservations
- Thoroughly familiar with automated data processing functions for passenger reservations
- Experienced in developing positive relations with customers and maintaining good customer relations
- Highly motivated self-starter interested in taking on new challenges

WORK BACKGROUND

1996–2003. Air Passenger Specialist, United States Air Force.

Completed special job-related training by correspondence through Air Force Extension Course Institute, Gunter Air Force Base, AL. Received excellent evaluations of job performance. Complete military record available on request.

REFERENCES

Complete reference information will be provided on request.

LUISA GOMEZ

Present Address   Permanent Address
46 Lafayette Street, #18   6800 Bayou Boulevard
New Orleans, LA 70118   Shreveport, LA 71104
Message: (318) 555-1265   (318) 555-8695

Objective: A position in public accounting utilizing my knowledge in tax accounting.

Education

A. B. FREEMAN SCHOOL OF BUSINESS, Tulane University, New Orleans, LA
Master of Accountancy degree, with an emphasis in tax, December 2001. GPA: 4.0

UNIVERSITY OF TEXAS, Austin, TX
Bachelor of Business Administration degree, with an emphasis in accounting and finance, May 2000. GPA: 4.0
- Dean's Honor List, Graduated with Distinction
- Beta Alpha Psi—National Honorary Accounting Fraternity
- Beta Gamma Sigma—National Scholastic Honor Society for Collegiate Schools of Business

Experience

A. B. FREEMAN SCHOOL OF BUSINESS, Tulane University, Baton Rouge, LA
Project Assistant (June 2000–present)

> Prepare monthly reports on university funds.
> Tutor students in Managerial Cost Accounting.

UNIVERSITY OF TEXAS PRESS, Austin, TX

Student Accountant (September 1999–April 2000)

> Prepared monthly managerial reports and financial statements.
> Maintained cash disbursements journal and performed bookkeeping.

INTERNATIONAL TRANSPORTATION, Mexico City, Mexico

Accounting Clerk (June 1991–July 1991)

> Performed data entry and bookkeeping.

Additional Information

Fluent in Spanish and Portuguese
Studied in Brazil for one year

JOSHUA GOLDSTEIN

205 Pendleton Street
Apartment 16-B
Americus, Georgia 31709
(912) 555-2918

CAREER OBJECTIVE

To obtain a position in service and repair of electronic data equipment

EDUCATION

Associate of Applied Science in Computer Electronics, Greenville Technical College, Greenville, South Carolina, 1995.

Additional training through U.S. Navy training courses at Combat Systems Technical School, Mare Island, California, 1996–1997.

RELATED EXPERIENCE

- Served as Data Technician First Class, U.S. Navy
- Performed general maintenance and repairs on computers, data link devices, and other electronic data equipment
- Inspected and tested equipment and components
- Diagnosed and repaired malfunctions in computers, data storage devices, and other equipment
- Performed troubleshooting and adjustment of electromechanical devices in digital systems
- Prepared maintenance schedules for electronic data equipment
- Effectively utilized various hand tools and electronic equipment

SPECIAL SKILLS/MEMBERSHIPS

Highly skilled in troubleshooting process

Member, Professional Electronic Technicians Association (ETA)

Currently undergoing ETA certification process

REFERENCES PROVIDED ON REQUEST

PATRICIA G. FRANKS

335 Canyon Drive
Bozeman, MT 59717
(406) 555-3490

EDUCATION

Montana State University, Bozeman, MT
School of Business
Bachelor of Science in Business Administration, 2001
Concentration: Finance and Accounting

ACTIVITIES AND AWARDS

Accounting Club
Dean's List
Letter of Appreciation, U.S. Marine Corps

EMPLOYMENT

Jones & Parker, Bozeman, MT, January 2000 to July 2000

Salesperson and Cashier, part-time
Assisted customers and oversaw cash register procedures.

Mountain Radio Group, Bozeman, MT, April 1998 to November 1999

Corporate Bookkeeper
• Reconciled monthly bank statements.
• Prepared monthly financial statements and bimonthly payroll for five stations.
• Managed accounts receivable and payable.

Quality Heating Co., Billings, MT, February 1997 to April 1998

Bookkeeper
• Prepared quarterly tax reports and bimonthly payroll.
• Managed accounts receivable and payable.

Jobs Unlimited, Boise, ID, May 1995 to January 1997

Credit Assistant
• Performed credit checks for new accounts.
• Managed accounts receivable.

U.S. Marine Corps, January 1992 to December 1995

Corporal

REFERENCES AVAILABLE

John R. Fleming, Jr.

4215 Pilot Creek Road
Clinton, MS 39058
(601) 555-7228

Career Objective

A position in aviation mechanics or a related field

Work Experience

- Served as Gunnery Sergeant (E-7), United States Marine Corps.
- Completed twelve years of active service concluding July 2002.
- Performed highest level tasks (Level 4) in helicopter maintenance and repair.
- Planned and scheduled activities of aircraft maintenance work centers.
- Performed a wide range of inspection and maintenance duties.

Training and Education

Certificate, Aircraft Maintenance, Lansing Technical College, Lansing, MI, 1991

Completed Marine Training courses in aviation mechanics (Air Ground Combat Center, Twentynine Palms, California), 1992 and 1997, and in personnel management (correspondence), 2000.

References Available

Robert A. Figueroa
2175 Broadway
Morganton, North Carolina 28655
(704) 555-3795
(704) 555-0908 cell phone/voice mail

OBJECTIVE: A senior management position requiring leadership, decisiveness, and vision.

PROFESSIONAL BACKGROUND

Career military officer, United States Army
Active service: June 1976–present
Rank: Major General

Career summary:

- Began service as a Second Lieutenant.
- Served as a combat infantry officer in South Vietnam.
- Progressed through officer ranks with consistently high evaluations.
- In addition to Vietnam, stationed in West Germany, South Korea, and several postings in the continental United States, including the Pentagon.
- Specialized in infantry leadership with secondary specialty in tactical/ strategic intelligence.

AWARDS/ACCOMPLISHMENTS

Received numerous medals, ribbons, and other recognitions including Bronze Star, Purple Heart, Meritorious Service Medal, and others.
Consistently earned praise from superior officers for outstanding performance.

EDUCATION

B.S., United States Military Academy, West Point, New York, 1976.
Graduated in top 25 percent of class.

M.B.A., University of Texas, Austin, Texas, 1984.
Completed additional studies at U.S. Army Command and General Staff College, Fort Leavenworth, Kansas, and at Army War College, Carlisle Barracks, Pennsylvania.

Additional details regarding Army career available on request.

References provided on request.

RICARDO ESTEBAN

105 Upland Drive
Sanford, FL 32773
(407) 555-4103

Career Objective

Responsible position utilizing my education and background as an experienced veterinarian

Professional History

1992–2003 Veterinarian, United States Army

- Researched animal diseases
- Inspected food to determine condition and quality
- Inspected cleanliness of facilities for food processing, meat packaging, and food storage
- Planned measures for controlling contagious diseases transmitted by animals or food

Veterinary Technician, White Animal Hospital, Tallahassee, Florida, (part-time and summers 1988–1992)

Performed basic support services including

- assisting in animal care
- kennel maintenance
- providing client support and related tasks

Education and Training

D.V.M., Florida State University, 1992
Special areas of interest: small animal practice research methodologies
B.S., Florida State University, 1988
Major: Biology
Minor: Physical Science
GPA: 3.8

Memberships

American Veterinary Medical Association
Florida Association of Veterinary Medicine

References available as requested

LISA ERDMAN

398 Berger Street
Medford, OR 97501
(503) 555-8007

OBJECTIVE

Position in payroll or other related business operations

MILITARY WORK EXPERIENCE

United States Navy, 1996–2002

Rating: Disbursing Clerk First Class (E-6)

Duties included the following:
- Maintained personnel financial records, including payroll
- Processed travel allowances and reimbursements
- Prepared correspondence and reports
- Processed vouchers for receipt and expenditure of funds
- Applied Navy regulations in computation of pay
- Prepared payroll checks
- Trained and supervised less experienced personnel
- Coordinated office work flow

TRAINING/EDUCATION

Successfully completed courses in the following:
- Keyboarding
- Office procedures
- Automatic data processing
- Payroll accounting
- Office administration
- Internal auditing
- Principles of supervision

REFERENCES AVAILABLE ON REQUEST

SHARON L. DUARTE

760 Hunters Mill Road
Helena, AR 72342
(501) 555-2624
E-mail: duartesl@xxx.net

CAREER OBJECTIVE: *A challenging role in human resources administration*

BACKGROUND

United States Coast Guard, 1988–2003
Job Specialty: Personnel Administration
Rank: Warrant Officer

RELATED SKILLS AND EXPERIENCE

- Performed a wide range of duties in personnel administration and general management
- Advised Coast Guard personnel (both enlisted and officers) regarding personnel regulations and procedures
- Supervised as many as eighteen workers in preparing and maintaining a comprehensive array of personnel records and accounts
- Prepared official correspondence and administered directives
- Provided leadership and oversight for various stages of office automation and computerization

SPECIAL SKILLS

- Highly skilled in analyzing policies and procedures and interpreting them for personnel at various skill levels
- Proficient in use of personal computers and LAN (local area network) systems for management purposes
- Skilled in effective communication, both oral and written

TRAINING/EDUCATION

Associate Degree, Trident Technical College
Charleston, South Carolina
Concentration: Business Administration

Additional education through Coast Guard training courses

REFERENCES AVAILABLE ON REQUEST

Linda Diaz Davis
708 Carson Road
Morganton, North Carolina 28655
(704) 555-3795 Home
(704) 555-0990 Cellular/Voice Mail

OBJECTIVE: A position in industrial security, hospital security, or a related area.

RELEVANT SKILLS AND EXPERIENCE

- Experienced in various aspects of protecting property and personnel.
- Skilled in performing physical security inspections.
- Familiar with effective procedures for reducing threats, anticipating security problems, and dealing with contemporary security issues.
- Skilled in using fire equipment, weapons, locks, alarms, and other devices and equipment related to security.
- Adept at various self-defense measures.
- Highly reliable in following orders, implementing procedures, and acting independently when needed.

WORK HISTORY

1994–2003 United States Marine Corps

- Completed basic training at Paris Island, South Carolina.
- Served as security guard at military installations including assignment at United States Embassy in Cairo, Egypt.
- Received several commendations for outstanding service.
- Decided not to reenlist after two tours of duty in favor of a civilian career in security.

EDUCATION

- Graduate, Security Guard School, Quantico, Virginia, 1996.
- Completed over 100 hours of language training, specializing in Arabic.
- Fluent in Spanish.
- Completed several correspondence courses and seminars related to security practices and procedures.

REFERENCES ON REQUEST

MARILYN DAUGHERTY

405 Warren Street
Mt. Pleasant, TX 75455
(903) 555-8631 (voice)
(903) 555-9091 (fax)

SUMMARY OF QUALIFICATIONS

Highly experienced in maintaining and repairing aircraft electrical, instrument, and power systems. Skilled and well trained in performing with efficiency and diligent attention to safety standards. Also experienced in effective management and supervision.

ACHIEVEMENTS

• Served effectively for a ten-year tour with the United States Navy

• Reached rating of E-7, Chief Aviation Electrician's Mate

• Demonstrated highly developed technical skills

• Worked with a variety of aircraft types

• Received excellent evaluations of performance

• Supervised over fifteen personnel

• Performed a variety of planning, management, and reporting functions

WORK HISTORY

1993–2003   United States Navy. Progressed from Airman to Chief Aviation Electrician's Mate. Served aboard U.S.S. *America.* Specialized in repair and maintenance of aircraft electrical systems.

1991–1993   Electrician's Assistant, Cox Electrical Service, Mt. Pleasant, TX.

EDUCATION

Certificate, Tidewater Community College, Portsmouth, VA, 1997 (included 18 semester credit hours in electricity/electrical systems).

Completed additional training at Naval Air Technical Training Center, Memphis, TN, 1993 and 1998. Courses covered electrical, electronic, and engine instrument systems; aviation weapons systems; physics; technical mathematics; and related topics.

REFERENCES

Available on request

LINDA T. COMBS

Public Relations Specialist
1906 First Street
Coast Mesa Beach, California 92626
(714) 555-3408

SUMMARY OF QUALIFICATIONS

- Energetic, articulate pubic relations professional.
- Skilled in all aspects of writing, designing, editing, and producing publications. Experienced in writing news releases, print ads, newsletters, and other material.

ACHIEVEMENTS

- Developed award-winning series of publications on career opportunities offered by U.S. Coast Guard (Gold Medal Award, California Public Relations Society).
- Completed writing, design, and layout for more than 100 Coast Guard publications.
- Initiated expanded community relations program designed to foster good relations with area businesses and civilian population.
- Designed and wrote newsletter for district personnel and their families.
- Received "Outstanding Communicator Award" from Long Beach Chamber of Commerce.

WORK HISTORY

1997–2002 **Public Affairs Officer**, United States Coast Guard, Fifth Coast Guard District, Long Beach, California

- Performed a wide range of duties related to pubic information/public relations. Wrote and designed brochures and other publications.
- Wrote news releases, ads, scripts, and other informational materials.
- Assisted in planning and implementing public relations/public information campaigns.

1995–1997 **Advertising Representative**, K & B Media, Long Beach, California

L.T. Combs—page 1 of 2

EDUCATION

B.S., California State University–Long Beach, 1999
Major: Public Relations
Minor: Journalism
GPA: 4.0 in major; 3.83 overall

A.S., Compton Community College, Compton, California, 1995

MEMBERSHIPS

Public Relations Society of America
California Public Relations Society

Larry Crowe
8 Progress Way
Apartment 2-B
Pearl City, HI 96782
(808) 555-3050

Summary of Qualifications

Highly experienced in servicing and repairing aircraft and pneumatic systems.

Skilled in inspecting, maintaining, and repairing hydraulic/pneumatic systems and systems components. Specialized in KC-130 aircraft.

Accomplishments

- Served as Aircraft Hydraulic/Pneumatic Mechanic, United States Marine Corps.
- Received excellent performance ratings. Earned several promotions, progressing to rank of Staff Sergeant (E-6).
- Mastered a variety of tasks related to servicing and repairing aircraft systems based on hydraulic and pneumatic principles.
- Used a variety of tools and equipment.
- Read and interpreted schematic diagrams, blueprints, and other diagrams.
- Reached advanced performance level.
- Worked independently.
- Provided supervision and instruction to those under me.

Employment History

Staff mechanic, Avis Aviation, 2001–present. Pearl City, HI.

United States Marine Corps, 1993–2001. Served at several bases with primary assignment at Marine Corps Air Station, Kaneohe Bay, HI.

Education

Graduate, Warren Wilson High School, Lansing, Michigan.

Successfully completed military training courses including United States Marine Corps correspondence course 13.45, Hydraulic Principles and Troubleshooting, offered by Marine Corps Institute, Washington, D.C.

References provided on request

Marie Chavez
312 Maple Drive
Perkinston, MS 39573
601-555-4785

Objective:

A position as an avionics technician with a commercial aviation firm.

Education:

Associate degree, Community College of the Air Force, 1997.
Additional training through Air Force technical courses.

Professional Experience:

1995 - 2002. Avionics Specialist, United States Air Force. Provided technical support for fighter aircraft.

1995 - 1998. 363rd Fighter Wing, Shaw Air Force Base, Sumter, South Carolina.

1998 - 2002. 23rd Fighter Wing, England Air Force Base, Alexandria, Louisiana.

Duties: Provided comprehensive maintenance and repair service for electronic systems and components of military aircraft. Developed familiarity with instrument systems, electronic warfare equipment, and other systems.

Performance:

Consistently received good or excellent evaluations. Helped achieve unit commendation award. Fully eligible for reenlistment but now prefer civilian career.

Complete military record and references are available on request.

Angela Caruso
1501 Welisford Street
Minneapolis, Minnesota 55455
(612) 555-1373

Education & Training

Certificate in Office Systems Technology
Des Moines Area Community College, Des Moines, Iowa, 1994

Additional training through completion of military courses and seminars

Professional Experience

1995–2002   Administrative Clerk, United States Marine Corps
Provided comprehensive clerical support services while serving as enlisted personnel in Marines. Stationed at Camp Lejeune, North Carolina.
Performed various duties including the following:

• Typed and word processed correspondence

• Maintained correspondence filing system

• Prepared documents including fitness reports, leave authorization, and identification cards

• Performed other clerical duties

Special Skills

Skilled in operating various types of office equipment

Adept in using contemporary word processing software, including Microsoft Word

References

Available on request

DAVID P. CARLETON
1404 HAYS AVENUE
WEST HARTFORD, CONNECTICUT 06117
(203) 555-7565 VOICE
(203) 555-9343 PAGER/MESSAGE

Summary of Experience

Ten years' experience in the United States Navy. Highly competent data processing expert. Knowledgeable and experienced in all aspects of data processing and information management.

Employment History

U.S. Navy, 1992–2002
Position: Data Processing Limited Duty Officer
Rank: **Lieutenant Commander**

Service Summary: Progressed from Data Processing Warrant Officer to Lieutenant Commander rank. Served as officer technical specialist. Performed bulk of service at Norfolk Naval Station, Norfolk, Virginia.

Duties: Performed a wide range of duties in providing electronic data processing services and supervising such functions.

Education

Bachelor of Science, North Carolina State University, Raleigh, North Carolina, 1992
Major: Computer Science

Additional training through Army training courses, including courses on management and supervision.

References

Available on request.

ANN MARIE BROWN

Apartment 3, Manorview Place
3000 Old South Highway
Providence, RI 02908
(401) 555-1895 (voice)
(401) 555-2498 (fax)

Objective

A rewarding position in journalism or public relations.

Highlights of Qualifications

- Fifteen years' experience in writing and editing for the U.S. Army

- A published freelance writer with articles in more than 20 magazines (complete list available on request)

- Experienced in photography as well as written journalism

Work Experience

1988 - 2003. **Journalist, United States Army.** Researched and prepared newspaper articles. Performed editing and layout duties. Coordinated public information activities, including development of news releases. Trained and supervised subordinates. Prepared and monitored budgets. Maintained contacts with representatives of civilian news media.

1987 - 1988. **Student Editor,** *The Daily Progress* (university newspaper). Wrote news stories and editorial copy. Assigned stories to student reporters. Performed layout and editing duties.

Education

B.A., Ohio University, Athens, OH, 1988
Major: Journalism.
Minor: Political Science
GPA 3.2

Memberships

American Society of Journalists and Authors
National Writers Club

References

References furnished on request.

William K. Brown
615 Cardinal Drive, Fergus Falls, MN 56537
(218) 555-0464 (voice)
(218) 555-1855 (fax)

Career Objective

A position in surveying or topographic engineering.

Related Skills and Experience
- Highly skilled topographic surveyor with fifteen years' experience in the United States Army.
- Achieved advanced skill level through extensive field experience and Army training courses.
- Thoroughly familiar with the most effective contemporary surveying methods, including use of various types of surveying equipment.

Work Background

As Army topographic surveyor, performed tasks such as the following:
- Recorded topographic survey data
- Operated a variety of survey instruments
- Performed topographic and geodetic computations
- Interpreted maps and aerial photographs
- Performed a wide range of computations including horizontal differences, angular closures, and triangulations
- Supervised other workers including topographic instrument repair specialists
- Supervised programming of electronic calculators
- Prepared technical and personnel reports

Training/Education

Completed military training in mathematics, surveying, engineering computations, technical writing, optics, data processing, and related areas.

References Available on Request

Michael Bleznakov
509 King Street
Evansdale, IN 47713
(812) 555-3618

Education

Bachelor of Arts, University of Kentucky, 1982.
Major: English Literature
Minor: Russian

Professional Experience

Intelligence Analyst for United States Army, 1992–2003.
Interrogator, United States Army, 1983–1992.
Rank: Major

• Performed a wide range of duties requiring strong organizational skills, analytical thinking, and persistence.

• Assembled, integrated, analyzed, and disseminated intelligence information.

• Handled and analyzed information collected from technical, strategic, and tactical sources.

• Supervised receipt, analysis, and storage of intelligence information.

• Compiled, edited, and disseminated intelligence reports.

• Assisted in providing general intelligence training programs.

• Supervised various personnel including interrogators.

Special Interests

Fluent in Russian language.
Highly interested in Eastern European affairs.
Willing to travel.

References and military record available on request.

Joyce H. Bishop
55 Rock Branch Road
Aurora, CO 80045
(303) 555-7954

Summary of Qualifications

• Experienced medical radiographer.

• Fully licensed and registered.

• Skilled in operating state-of-the-art radiographic equipment.

• Experienced in practicing effective patient relations and interacting with other health care staff.

Accomplishments

• Served as active duty personnel with the United States Army.

• Operated as a valued member of health care team at two Army medical facilities.

• Received three promotions in rank while on active duty.

• Worked effectively with both military and civilian personnel.

Employment History

1998–2003 *Radiologic Technician,* Fitzsimmons Army Medical Center, Aurora, CO 80045
Duties: Utilized X rays and other ionizing radiation for diagnosis and treatment of medical conditions. Served as technical assistant to radiologists.

1996–1998 *Radiologic Technician,* Walter Reed Army Medical Canter, Washington, D.C. 20012

Education

Associate of Applied Science in Radiography, 1996
Northern Virginia Community College
Annandale, VA

Completed additional courses (9 credit hours in health care management), 2000-2002
University of Colorado, Boulder, CO

Certifications/Memberships

• Fully certified (A.S., R.T.) by American Registry of Radiologic Technologists

• Licensed by Commonwealth of Virginia and State of Colorado; reciprocity in effect for other states

• Member, American Society of Radiologic Technologists

References

Available on request

James R. Bernstein
29 Appleton Heights
Spokane, WA 99258
(509) 555-0708

Employment Objective

A position requiring physical fitness, a strong work ethic, and the ability to work well independently or in combination with others

Experience

1998–2003 United States Army
Position: Infantryman
Rank: Corporal

- Served as an integral member of Army infantry unit
- Mastered the use of various weapons including machine guns and antiarmor weapons
- Served as team leader, directing deployment and employment of personnel
- Performed land navigation
- Collected and interpreted intelligence information
- Assisted in planning, coordinating, and reporting activities of subordinate units

Education

Diploma, Central High School, Spokane, WA, 1998
Additional education obtained through Army training

References available on request

MOHAMED BEHARI
11805 Boxwood Drive
Costa Mesa, California 92626
(714) 555-4160 (Phone)
(714) 555-4808 (Fax)
(714) 555-8764 (Cellular/Voice Mail)

CAREER GOAL

A rewarding position in dental technology

PROFESSIONAL BACKGROUND

Dental Laboratory Technologist, United States Navy.
Date of Service: September 1997 - January 2003

Duties: Performed comprehensive duties related to dental fabrication including the following:

- Fabricated basic dental prosthetic devices
- Made complete dentures, removable partial dentures, and fixed partial dentures
- Assisted in dental laboratory management
- Maintained inventory of equipment and supplies
- Completed administrative reports
- Implemented and coordinated quality control measures

EDUCATION/ TRAINING

- Graduate, U.S. Navy School of Dental Assisting and Technology, San Diego, California, 1998.
- Additional U.S. Navy courses completed in personnel management.
- Secondary School Diploma, The Carson School, Los Angeles, California, June 1997.

REFERENCES

Provided on request

Charles C. Beckman
1126 McGill Avenue, Apartment 13-B
Reno, Nevada 89557
Phone (702) 555-6719
Fax (702) 555-7629

Education & Training

Associate of Arts, Reno Community College, Reno, Nevada (General Studies)

Additional training through completion of Army courses and seminars, including language training

Professional Experience

Attaché Technician, United States Army
Rating: Chief Warrant Officer
Embassy Assignment: U.S. Embassy, Caracas, Venezuela
Duties: Provided general administrative and logistical functions in support of Defense Army Attaché office located in U.S. embassy.

- Managed and operated logistical support services

- Secured and managed housing for personnel assigned to the embassy

- Advised other personnel regarding protocol and matters of military courtesy

- Supervised enlisted and civilian support specialists

- Managed internal activities of Defense Attaché Office

- Performed other officer-level duties

Special Skills

Fluent in Spanish
Skilled in operating personal computers and basic office equipment

References

Available on request

Timothy C. Barlow

150 Howell Street • Aden, OK 74820 • (405) 555-2675

Objective

Position in warehousing, inventory, or general business where my organizational skills and personal efficiency can assist corporate goals.

Achievements & Experience

Served as an Aviation Storekeeper in the United States Navy, 1996–2003. Performed the following duties:

- Received, identified, stored, and issued aviation equipment and supplies
- Conducted inventories and maintained stock control records
- Used automated data processing supply procedures
- Maintained receipt control records
- Prepared various documents including requisitions, financial reports, and inventory records
- Prepared correspondence and messages
- Reviewed computer output for accuracy of records
- Received several promotions in rank, reaching the level of Aviation Storekeeper First Class (E-6)

Special Skills

- Skilled in using a variety of office equipment
- Adept in written and oral communication
- Able to function well under deadlines and other stresses

References and complete military record available on request.

J. Doyle Baines
200 N. Elm St.
Bedford, MA 01730

Objective:

A position in club management, restaurant management, hotel management, or a related area

Experience:

1999 - 2000 *Club Manager,* U.S. Army.
Rank: Warrant Officer.
Assignment: Officers' Club, Fort Lee, Petersburg, VA

Duties:
Performed a wide range of duties providing day-to-day management of officers' club. Coordinated purchasing and inventory of supplies. Coordinated food and beverage services. Supervised personnel. Achieved high performance ratings.

1996 - 99 *Assistant Club Manager,* Officers' Club, Fort Picket, Blackstone, VA

Duties:
Assisted club manager in all aspects of club management.

1994 - 96 *Waiter,* Twin Oaks Restaurant, 21 Ross Avenue, Bedford, MA 01730

Education:

Associate of Arts Degree, J. S. Reynolds Community College, Richmond, VA.

Additional training through Army courses including communication skills, food and beverage management, cost control systems, and personnel management.

References on request

Ben L. Adkins
151 Badger Street
Janesville, Wisconsin 53547
(608) 555-2402
(608) 555-5645 cell

OBJECTIVE:

Position in service and repair of radio equipment or other electronic equipment

ACHIEVEMENTS:

Served with distinction in United States Army.
Specialized in repair and service of radio equipment.
Military experience included duty under combat conditions (Persian Gulf).
Developed outstanding skills in identifying and repairing malfunctions.

WORK HISTORY:

1990–2002 Radio Equipment Repairer, United States Army
Served in Second Army, including the following assignments:
    Fort Bragg (Fayetteville, North Carolina)
    Saudi Arabia/Kuwait
    Fort Jackson (Columbia, South Carolina)

1988–1990 Sales Associate, Radio Barn, Janesville, Wisconsin

EDUCATION:

Graduate, Signal School, Fort Gordon, Georgia
Diploma, Manning High School, Janesville, Wisconsin
Licensing: Licensed amateur (ham) radio operator

REFERENCES:

Available on request

Matthew Slocum
E3 Apple Lane
Kensington, CA 94707
414-555-9085
msloc@xxx.com

Objective:

To obtain a position in Northern California that allows me to use my skills as a Web page designer and HTML programmer.

Education:

St. Thomas University, St. Paul, MN
B.A. in Communications and Technology, 2000

Related Experience:

May 2000–present
- HTML programmer, U.S.A. Communications, Oakland, CA
- HTML coder for all Web pages designed by U.S.A. Communications
- Account assistant for three large client Web sites

September 1999–May 2000
- Market researcher, Carey and Associates, St. Paul, MN
- Designed surveys and performed research to support client needs
- Developed a database system for processing research results

July 1998–September 1999
- Assistant editor, St. Thomas Weekly
- Assisted in editing, writing, and promoting a student weekly newspaper
- Computerized records and instituted financial reforms resulting in better stability and efficiency for the newspaper

1994–1998
- Computer Repair Technician, U.S. Army
- Serviced, installed, and repaired computer systems and related equipment
- Specialized in servicing computers supporting advanced communications equipment
- Received consistently high ratings from superiors

Matthew Slocum—page one of two

Awards:

P.E. Lilly Award for Outstanding Academic Achievement
Dean's List, each of four years of college

Skills:

- Programming Languages
  - C++
  - Cobol
  - HTML
  - Perl

- Systems
  - IBM
  - Apple
  - UNIX

- Software
  - Windows 98
  - Microsoft Word
  - Adobe Acrobat
  - Aldus Pagemaker
  - Adobe Photoshop
  - EXCEL
  - Filemaker Pro
  - QuarkXpress

References Available

Thomas H. Akers
1109 Old Depot Street
Stone Ridge, New York 12484
(914) 555-4124

Summary of Qualifications

Highly experienced sheet metal worker with seven years' experience in United States Army. Adept at using proper techniques for top-quality sheet metal work.

Highly dependable and productive.

Experience

• Served in United States Army, 1992–2003.

• Specialized in sheet metal work.

• Assisted in major projects including base expansion at Fort Lee, Petersburg, Virginia, 1994–95.

• Performed comprehensive duties requiring a broad range of sheet metal construction skills. These included

    —Fabrication and installation of air ducts

    —Installation of aluminum siding

    —Repair of various structures made of sheet metal

Education

Diploma, Washington County Vocational-Technical Center, Stone Ridge, New York, 1992.

Additional education through Army training courses.

References

Available on request.

Mario Kilde

1267 Buffalo Way
Pleasant Hills, MN 55408
(612) 555-1212

Objective: Position as a driver

SUMMARY:

- 10 years' experience in military as a driver of large and small vehicles on base and in city traffic
- Perfect driving and safety record
- Familiar with Twin Cities and surrounding areas
- Excellent health and personal strength, karate instructor at YMCA
- Personable, friendly
- High energy and very reliable
- Proven ability to produce within the confines of a demanding schedule

OTHER SKILLS AND EXPERIENCE:

Owner/Manager of Small Business
- Purchase and delivery of retail items, furniture
- Drove van for merchandise pick up
- Drove truck for wide variety of short trips in urban areas

Volunteer Driver, Big Brothers/Big Sisters
- Drove truck and fifteen passenger vans to transport groups of students in hundreds of weekly trips to sporting events and for field trips

Mail Handling
- Batched and sorted a large volume of daily mail for dental service company
- Handled important personal and business mail for clients of QuickMail Etc., including cashing social security and disability checks and paying bills

EMPLOYMENT HISTORY:

1990–2000 U.S. Army Driver, Fort Snelling, Twin Cities

1984–1990 Owner/Operator, QuickMail Etc., St. Paul, MN

1982–1984 Owner/Operator, Gifts and More, Minneapolis

1980–1982 Mail Handler, Twin City Dental Supply, St. Paul

EDUCATION:

Metro State University, 1978–1980
Coursework: marketing, merchandising, retailing, psychology

Complete military and employment records and references available on request

Antonia Harasmus
456 Shady Glade
Pepin, WI 54759
715-555-9898 home and voice mail
harasmus@xxx.com

EMPLOYMENT OBJECTIVE

To obtain a position in computer support services

SKILLS AND EXPERIENCE

- Experienced in writing, analyzing, testing, and implementing computer programs
- Competent in a wide variety of computer languages
- Expert inventor of interactive computer games for the adult market
- Qualified to conduct data systems studies involving meta-analysis techniques
- Skilled in advanced programming techniques
- Fluent in Spanish, including technical terms of the computer industry

WORK BACKGROUND

Programmer/ Analyst
United States Army
1998–2002

Computer Operator
United States Army
1994–1998

Video Gaming Consultant
Minnesota Technology Consortium
1992–1994

Youth Advisor to the Govenor's Task Force on Youth and Technology
Appointed by State of Wisconsin Governor Tommy Thompson
One of two young people asked to serve on task force from 1991 to 1992.
Helped write a proposal to improve computer access for young Wisconsinites through schools and libraries statewide. Proposal eventually became a bill and was passed in 1993.

Antonia Harasmus—page one of two

TRAINING/EDUCATION

Bachelor of Science, University of the Pacific, Sacramento, CA, 1992
Major: Computer Science
Minor: Mathematics

Army training courses at Information Systems Software Center, Fort Belvoir, Virginia

VOLUNTEER/TRAVEL EXPERIENCE

- Traveled in Latin America after graduation from high school
- Became fluent in Spanish and was trained as a medical aide by Catholic Charities in order to assist in emergency post-hurricane relief work
- Received Medal of Honor from Mayor of El Capitan, Peru

COMPLETE MILITARY, EDUCATIONAL, AND EMPLOYMENT RECORDS ARE AVAILABLE AT YOUR REQUEST

Donald B. Davidson

13 Williams Estates   **Home: 319-555-2354**
Cedar Rapids, IA 52406   **Mobile: 319-555-9087**

Summary of Qualifications

Experienced in operating a variety of construction equipment and other heavy and light equipment. Highly skilled in earth moving processes.

Accomplishments

Equipment Operator, active duty, United States Navy

• Operated multipurpose excavators and cranes

• Operated clamshells, backhoes, pile drivers, and other equipment

• Assisted in a variety of construction projects

• Advanced from Constructionman (E-3) to Equipment Operator First Class

• Earned excellent evaluations from superiors

• Held a perfect on-the-job safety record

Employment History

U.S. Navy, 1994–2002
Naval Construction Center
Gulfport, Mississippi

Cook Construction, 1992–1994 (summers)
Cedar Rapids, Iowa

Education

Diploma, South High School, 1992
Completed Navy training courses in equipment operation, safety, and related topics

References provided on request

KENDRA MACON
444 WEST DIVISION STREET
LAKE MARY, FL 32746
305-555-9032 (HOME)
305-555-6743 (CELLULAR)
kendra2@xxx.com

Objective
_____

Position with local printing press as assistant to warehouse manager, or similar position where I can be a productive liaison between the warehouse and management.

Summary
_____

- 4 years' experience in military press warehouse

- Hardworking, loyal, ambitious, eager to learn

- Able to view problems in a positive way and propose solutions

- Interested in streamlining operations and improving conditions

- Excellent working relations with warehouse staff

- Experienced liaison between workers and management

- Established uniform quantity of books per box at Hilltop, allowing for efficient stacking and shipping, more accurate inventory, and less damage to books

- Installed computer terminal at warehouse for immediate update of inventory

Education
_____

B.A., Liberal Arts, Florida State University, Tallahassee, FL, 1992

Employment History
_____

1996–2000	**U.S. Navy,** received several promotions in rank
1994–1996	**Warehouseman,** Hilltop Press, Cocoa Beach, FL
1992–1994	**Assistant Foreman,** Datalink Computer, Moro, FL

References, including complete military records, are available upon request

Sample Cover Letters

CARTER KATZ
474 East Triangle Street
Adrian, MI 49221
(517) 555-2686

July 16, 20--

Nancy Gregg, Human Resources Manager
Harris Corporation
P.O. Box 2929
670 South Mason Street
Indianapolis, IN 46204

Dear Ms. Gregg:

The enclosed resume is submitted in application for the position of Mail Services Manager as announced July 15.

Past employers have commented on my high-energy approach to work and life. I'd like to use my substantial experience in mailroom management to assist your mailroom with the types of duties described in the job announcement. As you will see, the responsibilities I fulfilled while serving in the military were very similar to those expected of this position.

I would be interested in meeting with you in person to discuss the position requirements and how I might address them. I would also be eager to provide letters of recommendation or any other details you might request.

Thank you very much for your consideration. I admire the outstanding image that your company has developed and hope that I can become a part of your organization. You can reach me at any time by calling the number listed above. I look forward to hearing from you.

Yours truly,

Carter Katz

SHAWNA A. JEFFERSON
238 Heather Avenue
Sioux City, Iowa 51104
(712) 555-0960 Home
(712) 555-7430 Cellular

November 29, 20--

Ms. Jenny Mitchell, Attorney at Law
Turner, Smith, Rose, and Mitchell
22 Appleton Building
4003 Smith Plaza
Pierre, South Dakota 57501

Dear Ms. Mitchell:

As you may recall, I spoke with you last year regarding possible employment with your firm following completion of my military duty. Now that my Navy career has concluded, I would like to express my interest in employment with your firm. Enclosed is a copy of my resume for your perusal. As you will note, I have had considerable experience in a paralegal capacity. It is my hope to build upon my military background by working in a leading law practice such as your own.

I would appreciate the opportunity to talk with you in person to discuss your firm's needs for paralegal assistance and how I might meet them. I would be happy to come to Pierre at any time, either to talk informally or to participate in a formal interview. Please let me know if I can provide additional information.

I look forward to hearing from you.

Sincerely yours,

Shawna A. Jefferson

RACHEL E. HUAN

275 Rolling Hills Drive
Toms River, NJ 08753
(201) 555-6622

March 6, 20--

George H. King, Owner
Rapid Printing, Inc.
P.O. Box 7112
Morristown, NJ 07963-7112

Dear Mr. King:

I am writing to inquire about possible employment with your company. I have seen your advertisements and am aware of the broad range of printing services you provide. I would be very interested in joining your staff should a position become available.

My background in the printing field includes four years' experience with the U.S. Army. Serving as a Printing and Binding Specialist, I performed a wide range of printing services. This includes operating various types of printing equipment while utilizing a teamwork approach in providing excellent service. I am enclosing a copy of my resume for your review. If you would like additional information, I would be glad to provide it. Please let me know if you would like to meet in person to discuss your employment needs.

Thank you for considering my resume. I hope to hear from you soon.

Sincerely,

Rachel Huan

Enclosure

Lisa M. Henry

532 Monitor Drive
Columbus, Ohio 43215
(614) 555-3987

August 18, 20--

Charles Metzger, President
Hoffman Enterprises
P.O. Box 344
Cleveland, OH 44102

Dear Mr. Metzger:

Please accept the enclosed resume and samples of my work in application for the position of Staff Photographer with your company. I am responding to the position announcement that appeared in the August 14 edition of the *Plain Dealer.* I have just concluded a highly successful tour of duty with the U.S. Navy. During this time I specialized in providing a wide variety of photographic services, and my photos received a great deal of acclaim from superior officers and others.

I am highly skilled in both color and black-and-white photography, effective composition, efficient darkroom techniques, and various types of specialized photography. I would be happy to provide additional examples of my work. I would also be willing to take on a sample assignment so that you can judge not only my abilities as a photographer but also my resourcefulness in completing assignments. Of course, I would appreciate an opportunity to meet with you in person and discuss the position more fully.

Please contact me if I can provide additional information. I look forward to the prospect of talking with you.

Yours sincerely,

Lisa M. Henry

ALLISON GOSNEY

206 Jeffries Drive
Riverdale, NY 10471
(212) 555-2013

September 12, 20--

Clifford Cox, Personnel Manager
First Flight Airlines
53 Airport Road
Wheeling, WV 26003

Dear Mr. Cox:

Thank you for taking the time to talk with me yesterday about employment possibilities with your airline. Your enthusiasm about First Flight is contagious, and I am highly interested in following up on our conversation.

Enclosed is a copy of my resume. You will see, as we discussed, that I have gained appropriate experience as an Air Passenger Specialist in the United States Air Force. In this capacity I performed a wide range of tasks in providing service for air passengers, and I also completed relevant job training.

I am a self-motivated employee who enjoys working with the public. I have excellent communications skills as well as strong organizational capabilities.

Please review my background and call me at the number listed above if you would like to talk further. I would be available for an interview at any time.

Thank you for your consideration.

Sincerely,

Allison Gosney

January 17, 20--

LISA ERDMAN

398 Berger Street
Medford, OR 97501
(503) 555-8007

Mr. Stanley Moore
Ames Construction
604 Dexter Avenue
Seattle, WA 98109

Dear Mr. Moore:

Have you ever wished you could find someone with an old-fashioned work ethic? Someone who knows the job and does it well every day? Past coworkers and supervisors have told me I am that kind of person. Please accept this letter and the enclosed resume in application for the position of Payroll Coordinator that was recently advertised by your company.

My background in payroll work, obtained though military training and experience, has provided me with a firm foundation in performing payroll functions and related business operational tasks. I am experienced in maintaining personnel financial records, processing vouchers for receipt and expenditure of funds, preparing payroll checks, and other key functions.

I would appreciate your review of the enclosed resume. Please let me know if I can become a part of your company's future. I will be glad to meet with you at any time to discuss employment possibilities with your firm.

Your consideration is appreciated.

Sincerely yours,

Lisa Erdman

June 1, 20--

ROBERTO A. REYES

1378 Orchard Street NE
Santa Fe, NM 87501
(505) 555-4056

Ms. Elizabeth Rowe
Human Resources Manager
Davis Manufacturing
5600 South Main Street
Phoenix, AZ 85009

Dear Ms. Rowe:

I am writing to inquire about employment opportunities with your company. Enclosed is a resume outlining my background and experience.

I am a self-starter with highly developed skills in implementing action plans, meeting goals, and providing leadership for other personnel. As my resume shows, my background includes not only the teamwork required in successful group endeavors, but also several years' experience as a Senior Sergeant. In this latter capacity, I worked closely with both officers and enlisted personnel, exercising a variety of management and leadership skills.

I would be interested in any position requiring teamwork and a strong work ethic. Please let me know if you have any openings for which I might apply. I will be glad to provide additional details or meet with you for a personal interview.

Thank you for your consideration. I look forward to the prospect of talking with you.

Sincerely,

Roberto A. Reyes

Craig R. Smith
104 Mount Tabor Road
Elizabeth City, NC 27909
(919) 555-2002

February 20, 20--

Alice Wilson, Personnel Manager
Charlotte Memorial Hospital-South
1134 South Highland Street
Charlotte, NC 28220

Dear Ms. Wilson:

I am writing to inquire about employment opportunities with Charlotte Memorial Hospital. Enclosed is a resume outlining my professional experience.

I have an extensive background in the area of medical records. I served for ten years as a medical records technician in the military, during which time I proved myself a highly reliable and productive worker. I have a strong work ethic and a penchant for accuracy and attention to detail.

My current objective is a position in medical records in a leading facility such as your own. I would be most appreciative if you would consider me for any openings, either now or in the near future. I would be happy to come to Charlotte for an interview at your convenience. I would also be glad to provide letters of recommendation or other information.

Thanks for your consideration. I hope to hear from you soon.

Sincerely yours,

Craig R. Smith

April 1, 20--

SHARON L. DUARTE

760 Hunters Mill Road
Helena, AR 72342
(501) 555-2624
E-mail: duartesl@xxx.net

Mr. Randolph Givens
Vice President
Allied Manufacturing, Inc.
Box 45447
St. Louis, MO 63123

Dear Mr. Givens:

This letter and the enclosed resume are submitted in the event that you may have a position vacancy in your personnel department.

I have a strong background in human resources management through my recent service in the United States Coast Guard. Over the past fifteen years, I have specialized in performing comprehensive duties in personnel administration and related management. During this time, I have proven myself to be a diligent and resourceful worker.

Should a position be open now or in the near future, I hope you will consider me. My resume provides basic details regarding my background and experience; if additional information is needed, please contact me by phone or E-mail. I would be glad to meet with you in person at any time.

Thank you for considering my application. I would appreciate hearing from you.

Yours truly,

Sharon Duarte

October 14, 20--

Mr. Wayne Burris
Director of Personnel
Ace Security Services
21 Jordan Avenue
Athens, GA 30603

Dear Mr. Burris,

I enjoyed our telephone conversation yesterday. Thank you for taking the time to talk with me. As we discussed, my background as a Marine security guard could prove a significant asset should I join your company. I believe I would bring a fresh perspective to your operations, and could help in your quest to make Ace an even more effective company.

I was especially interested to learn of your plans to expand your business internationally. My language skills and international experience should prove helpful in this regard.

The enclosed resume provides important details about my background. After you have reviewed it, please let me know if you would like to discuss present or future needs of your company, and how I might meet them.

Yours truly,

Linda Diaz Davis
708 Carson Road
Morganton, NC 28655
(704) 555-3795

ANGELA CARUSO
1501 Welisford Street
Minneapolis, Minnesota 55455
(612) 555-1373

July 11, 20--

Madison Life, Incorporated
415 Orleans Street
Chicago, Illinois 60610

Dear Personnel Manager:

I understand that your firm employs a number of word processing specialists, administrative assistants, and other clerical and administrative support personnel. I specialized in such functions while serving in the United States Marine Corps. Now that my military service has concluded, I would like to apply my skills and experience to the corporate world.

Enclosed is a copy of my resume. As you will see, I have a broad range of experience in providing office support services. I am a team player with excellent technical skills, outstanding communication capabilities, and the capacity to carry a heavy workload.

I would be most interested in discussing with you any opportunities for employment with your firm. Please contact me if you would like additional information.

Thank you for your consideration.

Sincerely,

Angela Caruso

December 6, 20--

COLLEEN QUINN
3104 Linden Court
Bradford, MA 01830
(508) 555-9576

Thomas Gaines
General Manager
Electronic Systems Technology, Inc.
210 Northview Drive
Amarillo, TX 79178

Dear Mr. Gaines:

Thank you for talking with me today. I enjoyed our telephone conversation. As you requested, I am enclosing a copy of my resume. This will provide you with specific details regarding my experience, training, and overall qualifications. You will see that I have a great deal of experience in servicing and repairing computer equipment, with special emphasis on advanced communications systems. My Army background has prepared me to work with a wide range of equipment, and I have proven to be a reliable, conscientious, and highly productive technician.

I would appreciate the opportunity to meet with you in person to discuss your company's needs for qualified technicians, as well as my capabilities for fulfilling them. Now that my military service has concluded, I am eager to take on a challenging position in the private sector. I will certainly appreciate being considered for any openings that your firm might have.

Thank you again for taking the time to talk with me. I look forward to hearing from you.

Sincerely,

Colleen Quinn

August 21, 20--

JASON RASKIN
1005 University Blvd.
Fort Collins, CO 80523
(303) 555-6922

William Anderson, President
Anderson Ford, Inc.
Box 2198
Boulder, CO 80301-2198

Dear Mr. Anderson:

I understand that your dealership operates a substantial auto body repair business along with the other aspects of selling and repairing automobiles. I am an experienced specialist in auto body repair and as such would like to offer my services should a position become available.

Enclosed is a copy of my resume. You will see that I have nearly ten years' experience in performing a variety of tasks related to auto body repair. Most of this experience came as a result of my military service, where I performed with excellence and received very positive evaluations from my superiors.

If a position opens with your company, I would appreciate being considered. I would be happy to provide additional information by mail or telephone or to come for an interview.

Thank you for any consideration you might give me regarding possible employment. I look forward to talking with you.

Very truly yours,

Jason Raskin

May 1, 20--

STUART PURDY, JR.

Route 4, Box 189
Winfield, Kansas 67156
Telephone:
(316) 555-0370 home
(316) 555-9676 cellular

Allison P. Smith, Vice President for Marketing
Bell's of Topeka
Topeka, Kansas 66603

Dear Ms. Smith:

As an individual eager to pursue a career in sales and marketing, I am submitting the enclosed resume for your review. I have a strong orientation toward the marketing function and would appreciate being considered as an addition to your staff.

My background includes both retail sales and extensive experience as a recruiter for the United States Army. In the latter capacity, I was fortunate to gain invaluable background in human relations, communication skills, time management, self-motivation, and other attributes necessary for successful marketing.

I am a hard worker who is willing to learn new skills and techniques. My positive attitude and emphasis on teamwork would be valuable assets for your organization. I would be very grateful for the chance to talk with you and further explore your company's needs. Please call me and let me know if we might arrange to meet.

Thanks much for your consideration.

Sincerely,

Stuart Purdy, Jr.

RASHEED B. SMITH II
11 Hillcrest Drive • Columbia, SC 29202
(803) 555-1859

March 31, 20--

Roberta Shumate, Director of Personnel Services
University of South Carolina
P.O. Box 1122
Columbia, SC 29202

Dear Ms. Shumate:

I enjoyed talking with you yesterday about the affirmative action program officer's position that was advertised in *The State*. Please let me reiterate my interest in the position.

Enclosed for your review is a copy of my resume. You will note that I have had significant experience in promoting affirmative action and conducting related personnel functions. My military experience has provided me a wealth of understanding in this area and given me the chance to work and live with a very diverse group of people. I believe I would do very well in the university setting and would be of service to others in the collegiate climate.

After studying the description for the position at your institution and discussing some of the details with you, I believe that my background provides a solid match with your expressed needs. I would be happy to amplify on my qualifications and interests through a personal interview.

If you would like to discuss this matter, please contact me by mail or telephone. I look forward to hearing from you.

Sincerely,

Rasheed B. Smith II

October 4, 20--

DENISE JACKSON-SMITH

906 Fairmeadow Townhomes
Dayton, OH 45469
(513) 555-6441 home/voice mail
(513) 555-9098 cellular

Douglas Sharpson
Medquip, Inc.
1033 Payton Avenue, South
Columbus, OH 43215

Dear Mr. Sharpson:

Would you like to be able to truly rely on your newest service technician, from day one? I am a quick learner, highly responsible, and a person who does things right the first time. As you can see from the three letters of recommendation requested by your advertisement in the *Post*, I have been highly praised by my coworkers and superiors alike.

Eight years in the military spent repairing, maintaining, and servicing medical equipment under all kinds of challenging field conditions has given me the confidence to state that I am highly qualified to join your team. My ability to work with diverse individuals has give me the people background needed to be a valuable team player.

Your company has been recommended to me by a number of friends who work in medical technology. I believe Medquip is a company that could give me the chance to build on my solid military background while contributing my unique skills to a high-tech, high service team.

I would be happy to provide more details or to come meet with you at your convenience. Thank you for your consideration. I look forward to hearing from you.

Yours truly,

Denise Jackson-Smith

November 13, 20--

Harrison Tillman
420 Reagan Road
Fort Smith, AR 72913

Mr. Andrew Davis
Division Manager
Superior Drug Stores
212 Imperial Place
Dallas, TX 75265

Dear Mr. Davis:

Enclosed is my resume for your consideration. I am interested in suitable openings in your chain of stores in the states of Arkansas, Texas, or New Mexico.

My Army training and work assignments as an assistant to pharmacists will make me a valuable addition to your operation. A position as pharmacy technician, assistant store manager, or a distribution support staff member would be appropriate to my skills and background.

I have a strong work ethic that will allow me to make a significant contribution to your company. Although I am currently enrolled as a full-time student, I am available for employment at the completion of the current semester. In addition, I would be happy to relocate.

Please let me know if you would like more information about my qualifications. I hope you will consider me for any appropriate position openings, and look forward to hearing from you soon. Thank you.

                              Sincerely yours,

                              Harrison Tillman